Roman Longoria

Designing Software for the Mobile Context

A Practitioner's Guide

Springer

Roman Longoria
Computer Associates Intl.
Three Memorial City Plaza
840 Gessner, Suite 600
Houston, TX 77024
USA

Series editor
Professor A.J. Sammes, BSc, MPhil, PhD, FBCS, CEng
CISM Group, Cranfield University, RMCS, Shrivenham, Swindon SN6 8LA, UK

British Library Cataloguing in Publication Data
Designing software for the mobile context: a practitioner's guide—(Computer communications and
  networks)
  1. Computer software—Development   2. Mobile communication systems
  I. Longoria, Roman
  621.3'8456'028551

  ISBN 1852337850

Library of Congress Cataloging-in-Publication Data
Longoria, Roman, 1969–
  Designing software for the mobile context: a practitioner's guide / Roman Longoria.
    p. cm.—(Computer communications and networks, ISSN 1617-7975)
  Includes bibliographical references and index.
  ISBN 1-85233-785-0 (alk. paper)
  1. Mobile computing.   2. Wireless communication systems.   I. Title.   II. Series.
  QA76.59L65 2004
  005.2'76—dc22   2003067312

ISBN 1-85233-785-0 Springer-Verlag London Berlin Heidelberg
Springer-Verlag is part of Springer Science+Business Media
Springeronline.com

Typesetting: SNP Best-set Typesetter Ltd., Hong Kong
34/3830-54321 Printed on acid-free paper SPIN 10965238

For my best friend Robin, thanks for your support and for bathing the kids while I worked on this book. For Austin and Diego, you provided the most wonderful distractions when I didn't really want to work.

Preface

Roman Longoria

The goal of this book is to provide a useful and timely guide to the practitioner who designs or develops mobile applications. The contributors to this book are leaders in the user interface (UI) community actively working in mobile platform technology and mobile application design. Thus, this book offers the reader unique insight into the latest technologies, market trends, design ideas, and usability data. We provide the reader with the latest information that will have direct and immediate impact on a broad scope of product design decisions, including those for voice, phone, and personal digital assistant (PDA) applications. In other words, this book is written by practitioners, for practitioners.

When I approached my coauthors about writing a chapter, I had only a few criteria. First, each author should have unique experience and expertise about a certain aspect of mobile applications. Second, that the authors be able to provide an introduction to the technologies with which they work. Third, that each chapter include case studies and lessons learned from empirical usability evaluations. And fourth, that each author include in the chapter some fundamental knowledge that they wish they had known when they got started designing for the mobile context.

As a result of this collaboration, this book offers the reader a unique reference to a broad range of mobile technologies, UI design principles, and tricks of the trade. The goal of this book is ultimately to provide a useful and timely guide to the practitioner designing or developing mobile applications. It is intended for user interface designers, usability engineers, developers, product managers, and others in industry who need a reference tool to understand what mobile technology can provide. It is also meant for students who want to build a strong foundation in technologies and their business applications.

The Mobile Context

Designing usable software applications has never been an easy task. It seems that just as we are getting a handle on designing good interfaces, the technology changes and we are faced with a new set of challenges. Software user interfaces have evolved from character based interfaces, to graphical user interface (GUI) desktop applications, to the Web and all of its facets. Modern wireless mobile applications are the newest wrinkle in the UI design landscape. Although applications running on mobile devices are by no means a new phenomenon, there is no question that recent technical advances have catapulted the mobile craze to a new, higher level. There are many challenges in designing wireless applications for mobile devices. Some of these involve parameters dictated by the hardware itself, the wireless transmission technology, and requirements specific to the applications themselves.

One hardware constraint is that text input is annoying at best. Entering data on a phone or PDA is tedious and requires a certain level of dexterity. Even new text input and handwriting recognition technologies do not really ameliorate the problem. Voice input may someday be a viable solution, but it is not yet perfectly reliable. To put it simply, applications that require text input annoy users.

Low bandwidth transmissions are also a hindrance. Slow download time seems to be second only to text input as a user annoyance. Most devices can download between 9 kilobits per second (Kbps) to 14 bits per second (bps) (no faster than a ten-year-old modem!). This makes every page count even more. Even with the promise of 3G technology, one should only expect downloads in the 40–60 Kbps range, despite the hype you may have heard of streaming video being just around the corner.

To make matters worse, designers and developers are faced with technology that is in constant flux, and users are faced with all of the idiosyncratic device specific differences in behavior. The devices themselves are often awkward or clumsy to hold, much less use, in a truly "mobile" context. In addition, there is no single industry platform, and there are no user interface standards or conventions that a designer can count on. Things become even more complicated when one considers the evolving combination of phones and PDAs.

Other challenges facing designers have to do with the applications themselves. Although the problems here are certainly related, or indeed imposed by, the hardware and technical constraints mentioned above, not all design challenges rest on the technology. There has been tremendous excitement and growth in consumer–oriented mobile services, but it seems that there still is a basic lack of understanding about what users want and need in mobile contexts. Just how much Web browsing or e-commerce do people want to do from their phones or PDAs?

As the title suggests, this book is about designing for a mobile context. I define this as any scenario in which a user is not in front of a computer (either a desktop or laptop). I wanted to keep this definition fairly broad, because the technology available is commensurately broad.

Trying to defining *the* mobile context is a difficult endeavor. Are users in a car, in a train, at the airport, on the golf course, on a yacht, on a sales call, at home? Are they walking, talking, sitting, standing, leaning on a bar, in well lit conditions or in the dark? You can never really know, and you cannot, and probably should not, design for all the possibilities. However, there are a few things you can count on. Users have a critical need for either information or to perform some task. This information or task is usually a very specific subset of what is available from the desktop. Users probably want to *get in* and *get out* as fast as possible.

Book Overview

This book will help you get started in the basics of phone, voice, and Web-based PDA applications. You are given unique insight to the latest technologies, market trends, and usability data that will help you make relevant design decisions. This book is not a complete, unabridged reference guide for designing mobile applica-

tions. No one book could cover that much information. However, you will take away
enough information to get started in a variety of mobile technologies. You will learn
what is possible in designs, and how to go about the process of making design decisions. References to other material that will expand on each technology are also provided throughout this text.

The first four chapters are authored by UI specialists working for companies
on the leading edge of mobile technology. Each author has a direct role in the design
and development of mobile platform technology and mobile application design.

In Chapter 1, the authors provide information on the mobile phone industry
as it transitions from 2G to 3G, with a focus on application environments and
devices. They discuss market trends for mobile phones, consumer characteristics,
and provide a thorough summary of mobile phone technologies. In addition, the
hardware characteristics of mobile phones are discussed with regard to how they
impact design decisions. Whether designing for Web-based or native phone applications, this chapter provides a impressive overview of what can be done. The
authors have extensive experience with Openwave and Kyocera, two companies who
pioneered the mobile phone user interface design.

In Chapter 2, a different mobile technology is examined. Voice application
design is discussed by two authors from Nuance, a leader in the voice technology
field. These designers provide a primer on what voice technologies can do, including speech recognition, verification, and speech-to-text. They start with a discussion
of the basic components of voice user interfaces (VUIs) and move on to describe a
design and development process that will help you get started on your own voice
application. Case studies are provided to provide insight gleaned from extensive
usability evaluations. VUI guidelines are outlined to help you avoid some common
mistakes.

Chapter 3 discusses the role that Java plays in mobile application design. Our
authors from Sun Microsystems discuss the Java™ 2 Platform, Micro Edition
(J2ME™), and how it enables mobile application designs. You are provided with a
technical discussion of a Java platform that fully leverages each type of device to
deliver a rich user experience. The chapter continues on with a breakdown of user
interface components and how to use them to construct an application. You are given
a foundation of the how the Java platform works, its requirements, and its potential
usage. This is essential information for those who will be designing applications for
this platform.

Chapter 4 introduces the reader to a new and exciting collaboration of technologies: multimodal applications. The authors discuss technologies at Motorola that
have blurred the distinction between cell phones and PDAs. The authors discuss a
user interface that allows multiple modes of interaction, offering users the choice of
using their voices or standard input devices such as a keypad or stylus. For output,
users can choose to listen or read. This new technology not only has accessibility
implications, but can simplify the user experience for all of us. However, like with
any new technology, there is a lot to learn, and this chapter provides a wealth of
information from two authors with extensive experience. Code examples are provided to help you get started with this technology.

The last two chapters are authored by UI specialists who have extensive experience designing enterprise and consumer applications. Heuristics and case studies

are provided to give you applied knowledge derived from the user-centered design processes used. In Chapter 5, the authors provide heuristics that apply to designing Web-based mobile applications. These heuristics are derived from iterative design cycles and usability testing at Oracle Corporation that yielded a wealth of ideas and validation data. Although this chapter focuses on enterprise applications, many heuristics can be applied to more consumer oriented applications.

Chapter 6 describes a process for developing user interfaces for advanced mobile, wireless devices. The process is based on contextual analysis, and prototyping, as well as on research conducted by Aaron Marcus and Associates, Inc., who designed future wireless mobile device user-interface concepts for Samsung Electronics (Korea) that combined the functions of mobile telephones and PDAs. This chapter walks the reader through the project phases, including design iterations, prototyping, and validation. An overview of the final product is then discussed.

Whether you are starting a mobile application initiative at your company or evolving the one you already have, this book will help you better understand the next generation of mobile technologies, and learn from the iterative design cycles from experts in the industry. If you are just starting out, we have some good news and some bad news. The bad news is that you are a few years behind the major software vendors who have been pursuing the development of mobile applications. The good news is that there has not been an extraordinary amount of enterprise acceptance of Web-based mobile applications, and you have not spent resources on obsolete technologies.

Computer Associates Intl.   Roman Longoria
January 2004

Table of Contents

Preface   vii

Chapter 1   Designing Applications for 3G Mobile Devices   1

1.1   Introduction   1
1.2   The Designer's Role   1
1.3   Understanding the Industry   2
1.4   Understanding the User   2
    1.4.1   Consumer Characteristics   2
    1.4.2   Consumer Devices   3
    1.4.3   Demographic Segmentation   4
1.5   Understanding the Technology   5
    1.5.1   Applications and Media Overview   5
    1.5.2   The Application Environment   6
    1.5.3   Symbian OS   7
    1.5.4   Brew   8
    1.5.5   Java   9
    1.5.6   Browser as an Application Environment   10
    1.5.7   Conclusion   11
1.6   Understanding Devices   11
    1.6.1   Designing for Local Applications   12
    1.6.2   Interaction Models   13
    1.6.3   Selection   14
    1.6.4   Device Interaction Models   14
    1.6.5   Scrolling   15
    1.6.6   Text Input Methods   15
1.7   User Interface Elements   17
1.8   When and What to Use (Markup, Native OS, or Messaging)   21
    1.8.1   Case Study: Games, Information Applications,
             Messaging Applications   21
1.9   Tips   25
1.10 Outtakes from Usability Testing   29
    1.10.1 Issue: Navigation   29
    1.10.2 Issue: Cost   29
    1.10.3 Issue: Login and Password   30
    1.10.4 Issue: Localization of Terms and Abbreviations   30
    1.10.5 Issue: Help   30
1.11 References   30
    1.11.1 Industry   30
    1.11.2 Market Research   31
    1.11.3 ISP   31
    1.11.4 Service Providers   31

1.11.5   Operator Requirements Documents   31
            1.11.6   Environments   31
            1.11.7   Device Manufacturers   31

Chapter 2 Designing Voice Applications   33

2.1   Introduction   33
            2.1.1   Some Background on Speech Technology   34
            2.1.2   Caller Satisfaction with Speech Systems   35
            2.1.3   How Speech Recognition Works   35
            2.1.4   The Elements of a Voice User Interface   38
            2.1.5   Design and Development of Speech Applications   39
2.2   Requirements Definition   39
2.3   High-Level Design   40
2.4   Detailed Design   42
2.5   Production   44
2.6   Tuning and Validation   45
2.7   Case Studies   47
            2.7.1   Overview   47
            2.7.2   Bell Canada   47
            2.7.3   Avon   48
2.8   Guidelines   52
            2.8.1   What Are the General Process Guidelines We Can Extract
                        from These Two Case Studies?   52
            2.8.2   What Design Guidelines Are Particular to the
                        Mobile User?   52
2.9   References   53

Chapter 3 Designing J2ME™ Applications: MIDP and UI Design   55

3.1   Introduction   55
3.2.   J2ME Platform Architecture   55
            3.2.1   Configurations   56
            3.2.2   Profiles   56
            3.2.3   Optional Packages   57
3.3   MIDP Overview   57
            3.3.1   MIDP Features   57
            3.3.2   MIDP Device Requirements   60
3.4   MIDP Application Overview   60
            3.4.1   Consumer Characteristics   60
            3.4.2   Characteristics of Consumer Products   61
3.5   Creating a MIDP Application   61
3.6   Using Abstract Commands   63
            3.6.1   Parts of an Abstract Command   65
            3.6.2   Paired Commands   66
3.7   Using MIDP User Interface Components   67
            3.7.1   High-Level User Interface Components   67
            3.7.2   Low-Level User Interface Components   74

3.8   Handling Deployment and Usage Issues 75
      3.8.1   Presentation Issues 75
      3.8.2   Size Issues 76
3.9   Conclusion 76

Chapter 4   Designing Multimodal Applications 79

4.1   Introduction 79
4.2   Motivation: Multimodal Interaction Use Cases 80
      4.2.1   Use Case 1: Multimodal Map 81
      4.2.2   Use Case 2: Multimodal Voicemail with a Smartphone 82
4.3   Discussion of Interaction Modes 82
      4.3.1   Graphical User Interface 83
      4.3.2   Voice User Interface 85
4.4   Contextual Information as an Input Modality 87
4.5   Degrees of Multimodality 87
4.6   Multimodal Synchronization: What Makes
      Multimodality Work? 88
4.7   Solutions for Voice and Graphical Interfaces 90
4.8   Design of Multimodal Applications for Mobile Devices 92
      4.8.1   Design for the Audience 92
      4.8.2   Social Implications of Multimodal Interfaces 93
      4.8.3   Design for Context 93
      4.8.4   Separation of Concerns 94
4.9   Internationalization and Localization 95
4.10 Usability 95
4.11 Design Artifacts 96
4.12 Testing Multimodal Applications 97
      4.12.1 Testing Strategies for Multimodal Designs 98
      4.12.2 Multimodal Testing Environments 99
4.13 Tutorial Example: Designing and Implementing a Multimodal
      Color Chooser 99
      4.13.1 Using SALT 104
4.14 Summary 106
4.15 References 107

Chapter 5   Heuristics for Designing Mobile Applications 109

5.1   Introduction 109
5.2   Summary of the Heuristics 109
5.3   Heuristics in Detail 111
      5.3.1   Heuristic 1: There Is a Need 111
      5.3.2   Heuristic 2: Every Pixel Counts 114
      5.3.3   Heuristic 3: Every Round Trip Counts 119
      5.3.4   Heuristic 4: Employ Feature Shedding 122
      5.3.5   Heuristic 5: Keep Your Navigation Model Simple
              and Clear 124
      5.3.6   Heuristic 6: Think Modular 126

5.3.7   Heuristic 7: Minimize Data Entry   126
5.3.8   Heuristic 8: Allow for Desktop-Based Customization   129
5.3.9   Heuristic 9: Fight the Hype   129
5.3.10   Heuristic 10: Basic UI Principles Still Apply   131
5.4   Conclusions   134

Chapter 6 A Development Process for Advanced User Interfaces
**   of Wireless Mobile Devices**   135

6.1   Introduction   135
6.2   Project Details   136
       6.2.1   Project Participants   136
       6.2.2   Project Dates   136
       6.2.3   Design and Development Process   137
6.3   Solution Details   140
       6.3.1   Design Concepts Based on User Observation   140
       6.3.2   Wireless Device Usage Space: An Analytical
                Framework   140
       6.3.3   Wireless Devices: The First Truly "Personal" Computer . . .   142
       6.3.4   The Promise of Mobile Computing   143
       6.3.5   Two Design Philosophies: Specialized Use vs.
                Does Everything   143
       6.3.6   The Design Concept Catalogue   143
       6.3.7   Input and Output Limitations   147
6.4   Post-Project Results   149
6.5   Acknowledgements   149
6.6   References   150

Index   151

Contributors

Chapter 1: Designing Applications for 3G Mobile Devices
Avril Hodges
Jolie Bories, Kyocera Wireless Corporation
Ronan Mandel, Openwave Systems

Avril Hodges has over 15 years experience in the User Interface field, specializing in design for consumers. She has shipped products for on-line shopping, on-line help, graphics and productivity; for mobile devices, pen environments, the WWW and the desktop. Avril was formerly responsible for managing usability testing of Openwave's products worldwide, and most recently was manager of the User Experience team in the Device Products Group at Openwave. Avril holds a Masters Degree in Communication and Graphic Design from the Royal College of Art in London.

Jolie Bories is a Senior User Interface Designer for Kyocera Wireless Corporation and spent 2 years working on the user interface for Nokia Mobile Phones. She has 8 years experience in user interface design for mobile devices and instructional software. She has written style guides, advisories, and requirements documents used by device manufacturers carriers, network service providers, and wireless content developers. Jolie has a B.S. degree in Cognitive Science from U.C. San Diego.

Ronan Mandel is the Senior Manager, Global Developer Services at Openwave Systems Inc. where he has run the developer services organization for the past 4 years. He is responsible for authoring style guides for HDML, WML, and XHTML-MP, as well as contributing several chapters to "WAP Development with WML and WMLScript" (2000). He has spoken about wireless application development in a variety of fora including Seybold, Comdex, Wireless Developer, SprintPCS and Cingular Developer conferences. Ronan holds a B.S. Degree in Geophysics from U.C. Santa Cruz.

Chapter 2: Designing Voice Applications
Jennifer Balogh and Nicole Leduc, Nuance Communications

Nicole Leduc is currently the Manager of the Usability Engineering team at Nuance, which she joined in 1999. She has been involved in user research and new product development for over 25 years. She is an expert on user-centered research and design methods, working within new product development teams to implement highly desirable high-tech services. Prior to joining Nuance, Nicole was Member of Research Staff for Interval Research, Assistant Vice President at Citibank, and Section Manager at Bell Canada. Nicole earned an MS in Communications from the University of Montreal in Canada.

Jennifer Balogh has been a Usability Engineer at Nuance Communications since 1998, where she has been designing and researching voice user interfaces for spoken

language systems. She has worked on projects for customers including Charles
Schwab, Fidelity, AT&T, British Telecom, and Citibank. Previous to Nuance, she
conducted language research at the Aphasia Research Center at the Boston VA
Hospital and was co-founder of Phaedrus Internet Development, Inc. Jennifer is
coauthor of the book *Voice User Interface Design* (in press), and has published
articles in journals including International Journal of Speech Technology and Brain
and Language. She holds a master's degree from UC, San Diego and is currently
working on her Ph.D in psychology.

Chapter 3: Designing J2ME™ Applications: MIDP and UI Design
Annette Wagner, Cynthia Bloch, Sun Microsystems, Inc

Annette Wagner is currently the human interface lead for the Java 2 Micro Edition
Platform (TM) in the Consumer Mobile Systems Group at Sun Microsystems, Inc.
For the last several years she has been working on designing and building Java tech-
nologies that are used in cell phones, two-way pagers, PDAs, screen phones, and
TVs. Ms. Wagner has over 20 years of experience in the user interface arena begin-
ning many years ago with the Apple Lisa computer.
Cynthia Bloch is a senior technical writer for the Mobile Information Device Profile
(MIDP) team. She has a master's degree in information science from the University
of Pittsburgh, and has worked as a software engineer and a technical trainer. Cynthia
is a co-author of the MIDP 2.0 Style Guide for the Java™ 2 Platform, Micro Edition
(Addison-Wesley, 2003), and has contributed to The Java Tutorial Continued
(Addison-Wesley, 1999).

Chapter 4: Designing Multimodal Applications
David Cuka, Bank of America
Tasos Anastasakos, Human Interface Lab, Motorola Labs

David Cuka received his Master's Degree in Computer Science from North Central
College. He has a broad background in the computer field with notable experience
with embedded systems programming, software engineering, domain engineering,
and technology transfer at Lucent Technologies. At Motorola, David led an
application development team to create Voice, Data, and Multimodal applications
based on Java and XML. At present, he works on software process at Bank of
America.
Tasos Anastasakos received his Diploma degree in Electrical Engineering from the
National Technical University of Athens, Greece and his Ph.D. in Electrical and
Computer Engineering from Northeastern University, Boston, MA. While completing his Ph.D. degree, Tasos was a Research Assistant at BBN Corporation. The
results of his dissertation on "Speaker Adaptive Training" have been widely adopted
in the development of large vocabulary speech recognition systems. Currently, Taos
is a Distinguished Member of Technical Staff at Motorola Labs. He is leading a
project effort on multimodal interfaces for mobile devices and is representing
Motorola Labs in the W3C Multimodal Integration Working Group.

Chapter 5: Heuristics for Designing Mobile Applications
Roman G. Longoria, Computer Associates Intl.
Mick McGee, Eric Nash, Oracle Corporation.

Roman Longoria received his doctorate in Human Factors and Industrial Psychology from Rice University. He has over 13 years of Human Factors and Applied Psychological research and design experience working with NASA, the US Air Force, and the software industry. He served as a Principal with Oracle Corporation's Usability and UI Design Group where he was responsible for the design of mobile applications and platforms. He holds the status of a Certified Professional Ergonomist. Currently he is the Director of User Interface Design for Computer Associates International.

Mick McGee received his doctorate in Industrial & Systems Engineering from Virginia Tech University. Currently, he is Mobile UI Lead in Oracle's Usability and Interface Design Group; as well as Chair for the Human Factors and Ergonomic Society (HFES) Communications Technical Group. His primary interests are in designing and evaluating interfaces for advanced information displays (neural, voice, mobile, virtual, tele, and desktop).

Eric Nash received his masters in Industrial Engineering from Virginia Polytechnic Institute and State University. He has 4 years of Human Factors research experience and 5 years working within the software industry. He currently works as a Usability Engineer with Oracle Corporation's Usability and UI Design Group.

Chapter 6: A Development Process for Advanced User-Interfaces of Wireless Mobile Devices
Aaron Marcus, Aaron Marcus and Associates, Inc. (AM+A).

Aaron Marcus is the founder and President of Aaron Marcus and Associates, Inc. (AM+A). He is a graduate in physics from Princeton University and in graphic design from Yale University. Mr. Marcus has written over 100 articles and written/co-written five books, including (with Ron Baecker) Human Factors and Typography for More Readable Programs (1990), Graphic Design for Electronic Documents and User Interfaces (1992), and The Cross-GUI Handbook for Multi-platform User Interface Design (1994) all published by Addison-Wesley. He has published, lectured, tutored, and consulted internationally for more than 20 years and has been an invited keynote/plenary speaker at conferences of ACM/SIGCHI, ACMSIGGRAPH, and the Human Factors and Ergonomic Society. He is a visionary thinker, designer, and writer, well-respected in international professional communities, with connections throughout the Web, user interface, human factors, graphic design, and publishing industries.

Chapter 1

Designing Applications for 3G Mobile Devices

Avril Hodges, Jolie Bories, Ronan Mandel

1.1 Introduction

This chapter provides information on the mobile phone industry as it transitions from 2G to 3G, with a focus on application environments and devices. This does not attempt to tell *how* to design mobile applications, but offers an overview on what to be aware of when designing content and applications. While the information here is specific to mobile phones, and does not cover other devices such as PDAs or communicators, awareness of physical and technological constraints of any device type is an essential starting point in the design process.

1.2 The Designer's Role

In working with mobile devices, the user interface design role may take one or more of the following forms:

- Employee working directly for a device manufacturer on native or embedded applications
- Third party content developer (for software integration or download)
- Network service provider creating requirement documents or user interface style guides

Depending on the role, there are various issues to consider. For example, when designing content or applications for a device, the designer must be aware of hardware properties including fixed and programmable keys, graphical display, and user interface style. In addition to the device properties, a third party content developer must be aware of the development environment as well as the device key, screen, memory, and file format constraints available on the device. Individuals writing requirements and style guides must be aware of the technology for a specific application and overall device capabilities. For browser-based applications, it is important to know what interaction and navigation model and graphical presentation the browser supports (such as optional properties in the standard, as well as font and image formats). Similarly, for other downloadable content, it is important to know what file types are supported.

1.3   Understanding the Industry

There are many factors to consider when designing for mobile phones. Region, technology, and customer diversity must be taken into account, along with trends and adoption patterns. For example, in Europe in 2002, upward of 24 billion SMS messages were sent monthly, and SMS was the most popular secondary phone feature. European GSM networks allow sending and receiving SMS between service providers, although the creation and display of message content is device dependent. In the United States, SMS was ranked tenth in popularity, after Web access and voice-activated dialing. This reflects a market fragmented by technology where CDMA, TDMA, and GSM networks compete for subscribers, resulting in interoperability issues between service providers. As these interoperability issues diminish, there will be opportunity for growth in messaging services.

Figure 1.1 shows distribution of subscribers by technology. GSM represents the major segment, and will continue to dominate markets until the transition to the 3G technologies of W-CDMA and CDMA2000 are complete. It is anticipated that Asia-Pacific will experience faster growth than in the other world markets, both in terms of subscribers and deployment of 3G technology. See Figure 1.2.

1.4   Understanding the User

1.4.1   Consumer Characteristics

Ease of learning and ease of use are essential to the success of consumer products. Users bring a plethora of expectations and mental models to bear when they encounter new products, especially if they have acquired an item based on advertising hype about advanced features ("It slices, it dices, it'll do your taxes"). Consumers want a device to work intuitively out of the box. They will probably not read the manual beyond the basic instructions, if at all, and will not remember how to use advanced features. So it's not surprising that they are intolerant of hard-to-use products and will return or stop using these products if they are frustrated with the experience. Consumers don't hesitate to give the product bad word-of-mouth to friends and relatives, reducing the likelihood that others in their circles will buy the same thing. For example, it's not unusual for teen peer groups to have a de facto technical leader, often a dominant personality in the group, who informally screens devices for coolness, style, ease of use, and compatibility, and often influences device and service plan selection for peers. The group shares information about

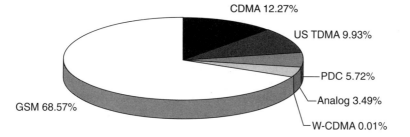

Figure 1.1 World cellular subscribers by technology, June 2002 (source: GSM™ World)

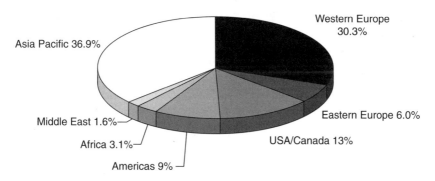

Figure 1.2 World cellular subscribers by region, June 2002 (source: GSM™ World)

upgrades, cool (especially free) stuff such as ring tones, screen savers, and images, and ways to get better mileage from devices.

Business users can expect to receive on-the-job training or take tutorials to use job-related products, and can always ask colleagues for advice when they have difficulty. But business users are also consumers when buying for themselves.

1.4.2 Consumer Devices

The characteristics of a "consumer device" are:

- Bought by an individual for personal or immediate family use, as opposed to being supplied by an employer for job-related activity
- Has a specific primary purpose (for example; a phone's primary purpose is for making and receiving voice calls)
- Additional features mustn't interfere with or over-complicate the primary use
- Must be easy to use out of the box with minimal reference to an instruction manual

While many consumer devices are purchased for advanced features, they are more often used only for the primary functions.

Example: VCR.

On early VCRs, consumers had difficulty setting or resetting the clock/timer when the device had been disconnected from a power source. With the system clock not set, the unit couldn't identify when to start or stop a recording, and in addition, the flashing LED drew attention to owners who were inept at controlling the device. (This is typified in the cliché of the flashing LED displaying 12:00:00.)

The final action in the sequence to set the pre-record feature required turning the device off. This was so counter-intuitive that many users failed to use the feature successfully, resulting in the majority of VCRs being used solely to record manually in real time, or to play pre-recorded videos.

1.4.3 Demographic Segmentation

While income levels and other factors are significant for many markets, the dominant demographic segmentation for mobile phones users is by age, as shown in Table 1.1.

Consumers and business users can also be differentiated by the secondary use of their device. See Table 1.2. "Business users" refers to a category who acquired a device and are using it mainly for business-related activity. As of 2002, this group made up 9% of subscribers in the US. For usability testing purposes, be aware that other uses may play a significant role in device choice. Ask users to describe all the ways they use their phones.

Table 1.1   Cellular phone demographic groupings

Group	Ages
Pre-teens	10–12
Young teens	13–15
Older teens	16–19
Young adults	20–25
Adults	26–35 36–49 50+
Business users	–

Table 1.2   Mobile phone features by primary and secondary use

Primary telephony use	Consumers	Business users
Making and receiving voice calls	X	X
Voicemail	X	X
Secondary telephony use		
Conference calls		X
International roaming		X
Call transfer		X
Priority line		X
Other secondary use		
Text messaging (SMS)	X	X
Games	X	
Calendar and address book synch with desktop		X
E-mail		X
Intranet access		X
Internet access (travel updates, restaurant guide, entertainment)		X
Fax		X
Other activities		
Ring tones	X	
Wallpapers, screen savers, images	X	
Picture messaging	X	
MMS	X	
Push services (sports scores, travel, infotainment)	X	X

1.5   Understanding the Technology

1.5.1   Applications and Media Overview

There are two main categories of applications that can be developed for mobile devices. The first includes applications that reside and run on the device.

Applications that run locally on the device can either be preloaded in the device or downloaded via a cable from a computer, pushed to the device, saved from a Web/WAP site, or downloaded using a mechanism such as Open Mobile Alliance (OMA) download. Such applications may be developed in Java, Brew, Symbian, or for the specific device operating system, and may include games, images, ring tones, and messaging templates.

The second category includes applications that reside on a server and run through the device's browser. Applications that are browser driven may support content written in WML, cHTML, XHTML, HTML, and so on. Depending on the device, the integrated browser may support one or any combination of these languages.

When designing and developing content, it is important to note that downloaded applications that run directly on the device can be rich – meaning the content developed can be made more powerful and take advantage of the device's capability, and can be faster because they may run directly off the device's processor. Browser-based applications are less flexible due to the limitation of the markup language, but because the browser processes the markup language, less development work may be required, as a single application may run on a variety of devices. However, content may still need to be customized for the various browsers. Data applications are often slower because they rely on network speed and connectivity, but are more suitable for frequently changing information, such as sports scores or traffic information. In both cases, content developers need to focus on different device and browser properties to optimize the user experience.

1.5.2   The Application Environment

There are a number of significant technology questions that must be answered when developing applications for 3G, above and beyond simple device constraints. The most immediate question is the environment in which an application will execute. The environment can be defined on a number of different dimensions, some of which are in the control of the developer, while some constraints are placed either by the device or the network on which it runs. Developers can build applications that run as a local executable on the device, with or without access to network resources. A simple single player game would be a local application not likely to require access to network resources. But a chat application where the executable resides on the handset would clearly rely on network access for sending and receiving messages. Alternatively, applications can be structured as markup or browser-based where processing and logic are all controlled on a server, and presentation and interaction are accomplished in a pre-installed browser. Many popular instant messaging services offer browser-based interfaces for wireless devices architected in such a way that all processing is done on the messaging server itself.

Perhaps the most feature-rich applications built for 3G will be those built to run locally on the device. The 3G environment represents a step forward for developers as operating systems become more robust and powerful and over-the-air download mechanisms for applications are widely available. In addition, devices will also continue to ship with some set of pre-loaded applications such as messaging clients, browsers, phone books, and games which may (or may not) be possible to supplement or replace. This class of application will run on the native operating system (OS), and when building programs to run natively, developers have little choice over the programming language that must be used. Tools, sample code, compilers, and the device properties for native applications usually must come directly from the device manufacturer and the application must be tested and ported to the specific device.

Applications written to the native OS are generally built using compiled languages such as C or C++. There are many advantages to building applications to the native OS. Often such applications will run more rapidly and smoothly, and can gain secure access to local device resources, which may not be possible with other types of application environments. For example, a native application may have access to the local phone book to pick or add a number, and may also be able to gain access to the device serial ports to accomplish tasks such as printing or beaming data over infrared (IR). In general, any tasks the hardware of a device is capable of accomplishing may be accessible by a native application. However, device manufacturers may not expose certain application programming interfaces (APIs) or features for security reasons. These decisions are made largely on a manufacturer-by-manufacturer basis.

The downside to building native applications is that there must be a separate executable built for each device. Compilers and development environments for a given device may be difficult to obtain, and will likely have to come directly from the manufacturer. There may also be specific image or media formats supported natively (e.g., SiS or eAmimator) for which tools must be obtained. Applications built to a native OS often must be pre-loaded before the device is placed in the box for retail sale, or via a software download (sometimes called flashing) that can be accomplished only by a retail outlet.

1.5.3 Symbian OS

Devices built on the Symbian OS allow developers to build native applications without the need for direct interaction with a device manufacturer. Development tools are widely available with a listing on the Symbian developer site (see References). While an application built on the Symbian platform may need to be opti-

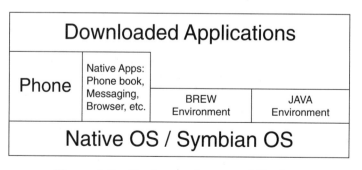

Figure 1.3 Device systems architecture

mized for the specific device, there is not a need for a complete redevelopment effort. As a rule of thumb, porting a Symbian application from one device to another comes down to an 80/20 rule, where 80% of the code base can stay intact, while 20% will need to be modified to fit the layout of the new device.

Increasingly, more device manufacturers are licensing a user interface module on top of the Symbian platform developed by Nokia called Series 60. This interface module is targeted primarily at "one-handed smart phones," and has been licensed by other device manufacturers such as Samsung, Siemens, and Panasonic. The goal is to reduce that last 20% porting effort required by Symbian application developers to get programs working seamlessly across multiple devices. Symbian OS devices are largely found in the GSM community, and phones running it have been shipping in European markets since late 2000 (based largely on membership in the Symbian consortium), but the operating system is penetrating other 2.5 and 3G markets.

For applications that are designed to run locally on a handset, but not ship with a device at point of purchase, there are three different application development environments to weigh: Symbian, Java, or Brew. The decision as to which environment is supported will be made by a device manufacturer, and application development will be constrained by this. We have already touched briefly on Symbian OS applications, which represent perhaps the only "lower layer" environment that allows for application downloads. The next level up in the application environment is represented by Brew and Java.

1.5.4   Brew

Brew is a language and environment developed and licensed by Qualcomm. The Brew environment is embedded into the Qualcomm CDMA chipset, and provides developers with a C++ based environment. Applications written in Brew may be able to gain access to system resources such as the device call manager, or the local ring tone storage repository. The development environment of choice for building Brew applications is Microsoft Visual Studio.

Brew has become a compelling environment for developers partially based on the business model that Qualcomm has established. Developers must go through an arduous certification process to enable the over-the-air download of their applications, but once this is accomplished, and a relationship established with Qualcomm, there is no need to negotiate directly with a service provider for distribution. This is a sound model for applications targeted at consumers, such as games or ring tones, but for vertical or enterprise developers who wish to simply build applications for use within their corporation, this distribution environment is unnecessarily restrictive. Another limitation of the Brew environment is that it is today only available in CDMA markets. Again, developers may not have the choice of any other client application environment, because it is available on the device and decisions are made by the wireless service provider.

1.5.5   Java

Java is an interpreted language that has gained significant ground on mobile phones in recent history. Improvements in processing power and performance of the virtual machine have led to Java being a viable environment for local applications.

The Java environment that will most likely be deployed is the MIDP (Mobile Information Device Profile), which is a set of Java classes targeted at mobile phones. There is a critical mass of devices that support MIDP, and applications can be developed using the wide variety of Java development environments available on the market. Device manufacturers also make emulators available which plug into many IDEs (Integrated Development Environments) for application testing and development purposes. Java applications can be downloaded to devices either via a serial cable, or more commonly, over-the-air. Over-the-air download, or "MIDP OTA" is a process wherein a descriptor file is first downloaded from a mobile device via a Web browser. This descriptor is simply a text file containing some basic properties about the application, along with a Uniform Resource Identifier (URI) for the download of the executable package. Once the executable package is downloaded and installed, it is executed and managed in a local environment on the device. This local environment has many security restrictions, so that applications may not access native applications or even other Java applications on the device. While this application "sandbox security model" provides end-user security, it also means that application capabilities are limited.

While there is a standard specification for MIDP that is guided by the Java Community Process, many device manufacturers extend the functionality available in the Java environment on their devices through custom classes and APIs. These may include classes for sounds, graphics, network access, and perhaps even access into the local phone environment.

Additionally, a given device with a Java Virtual Machine may (or may not) support any number of Java Service Requirements (JSRs) that provide services above and beyond the MIDP specification, from sending SMS messages, to accessing a camera in a device, to XML processing. While the promise of Java is "write once, run anywhere," application developers must make decisions about the level of functionality for their applications since many of the proprietary and JSR extension classes offer compelling features, but are not available on all handsets. At the same time, even if a developer adheres strictly to the MIDP standard, applications may have to be optimized for display on any given device.

Some of the main advantages to building applications in a Java environment are the openness of the language, wide availability of tools, low barrier to getting code onto a real device, and prevalence of the Java environment (Java interpreters run on top of Brew and Symbian too!). Device manufacturers and network service providers have lined up behind the language and are giving it full support. Java development environments can be obtained from Motorola, Nokia, and Siemens (among others), and Java application tools can be found on service provider Web sites such as SprintPCS, AT&T Wireless, and Vodafone. See References.

Applications built in any of the environments above are not restricted to running locally on a device. Each language provides interfaces to a networking stack so that data can be exchanged and requests made across a network. The classes provided are generally lower level classes, which allows the exchange of data in ANY format over a network connection. This opens up the possibility for building applications that handle streaming media, parse arbitrary XML data, or execute asynchronous transactions. The ability to establish a network connection from a local application environment means that applications are not limited to the resources they come with upon installation. However, due to security reasons, it may not be possible to download new executable modules, only data to be handled, stored, or managed locally.

1.5.6   Browser as an Application Environment

The browser resides locally on the device, and applications written for the browser must be tailored to its capabilities. For example, in most markets there are many devices that support a WAP browser, but the specific version of WAP will determine what features and markup language that browser supports. While the WAP1.1 and 1.2 standard requires devices to support markup in WML, WAP2.0 standard permits applications to be written in either WML or XHTML.

There are also many optional features available within the WAP standard, such as most CSS properties, fonts, and media formats. Since the WAP standard does not mandate a specific user interface model in the browser, content may render slightly differently between browsers and/or devices. However, with the use of XHTML, there are fewer inconsistencies across navigation models than seen in WML applications.

One issue to be particularly aware of concerns text input. On some devices text input may be inline and on another the user must select the text field, which opens another window or screen for text entry. In the latter case, if the referring text provided some description or format explanation (e.g., Birth date: (dd/mm/yyyy)), this information and formatting may disappear when the new window or screen is displayed. Fortunately, some wireless service providers are requiring browser vendors to support a more common look and feel for specific optional features. Refer to target device/wireless service provider developer sites for more information and/or style guides on what standard, formats, and features the device supports. At the end of the day, applications that are built to the specific characteristics of a given device are going to provide for an optimal user experience.

Web-based applications that run on a PC are sometimes designed for a specific browser (e.g., Netscape Communicator or Microsoft Internet Explorer). Similarly, when developing applications for mobile devices, content should be written to the browser, with less emphasis on the device itself. That is because the browser application has its own interaction model built in. When designing a browser application, the focus is on the markup version and other properties that particular browser supports. For example, WAP standards do not define a presentation model and much of the CSS properties are also optional. However, there are some service providers who require device manufacturers and browser vendors to implement a specific set of properties. Refer to service provider and browser vendor style guides and SDKs to learn more about what is supported.

Even though an application is written for a specific browser, it should also be optimized for certain devices. For example, the screen size, file type, and bit depth between devices may differ, so instead of having the browser or device resize the image to fit the screen, images should be tailored for those specific metrics. Also, take note of the available font size because this can make a difference when creating and using icons that fit the same line height. The WAP standard makes WAP Pictograms an optional feature of many browsers; however, for those browsers that do support them, this will make use of the optimal size and will enable quicker presentation of the content since the icons reside in the device rather than requiring them to be downloaded.

1.5.7 Conclusion

When designing and developing content, it is important to note that downloaded applications that can run directly on the device can be rich – meaning the content developed can be made more powerful and take advantage of the handset's capability. They may be faster because they are not interpreted as Java or markup-based applications must be.

Markup-based applications are less flexible in terms of what they are able to do and they run slower because they are reliant on network speed and connectivity. They are best suited for applications that require frequent updating, such as sports scores, traffic reports, and chat sessions.

Markup-based applications can be written once to run on many devices, but still may need to be customized for the various browsers. When designing and developing content for either environment, content developers need to focus on different device/browser properties to optimize the user experience.

1.6 Understanding Devices

The feature set for most devices within a market is largely the same and may be specified by the network service provider. Depending on the market, some service providers may have a list of requirements that the device manufacturer must fulfill in terms of features, presentation, navigation, and even the physical aspects of the device itself. In other markets, the service provider may have a list of features and high-level requirements that need to be fulfilled in terms of general properties for a given feature. However, even with service providers submitting requirements, device manufacturers can differentiate their handsets from others in several ways including those shown in Table 1.3.

Many device manufacturers see user interface as one of the most important brand differentiators and strive for consistency within products and/or product lines. For example, a device manufacturer may have a look and feel for a specific product based on the hardware of the device, but may also have a general look and feel in terms of graphics, menu structure, and language use for all their products, in order to maintain consistency. To device manufacturers, consistency is what drives brand loyalty, and market share retention or growth occurs if a user is familiar with their

Table 1.3   Device product differentiators

Quality	Sound Network coverage Robustness Battery life Brand
Hardware design	Industrial design Size Weight Screen size Key layout Ease of pressing buttons Integrated or attachable devices (Camera AM/FM radio, MP3 player, Bluetooth)
User interface	Feature set Interaction (key mapping) Navigation (hierarchical and between applications) Localization
Personalization	Changeable faceplates or keypads Downloadable objects (images, sounds, games, applications) Customizable ring tones Customizable/downloadable themes

devices and buys or recommends the brand to others based on ease of learning and use.

When designing for mobile devices, there are several issues that are common to applications regardless of whether they are native or downloaded. These include:

- Screen size
- Bit depth: color, grayscale or black and white
- File formats for image, sound, and video
- Memory allocation for browser content or applications
- Input mechanisms: available character set, keys for inputting letters, symbols, and numbers, and field formatting

1.6.1   Designing for Local Applications

Device Properties

The transition from 2G to 3G devices is often associated with data connectivity speeds. From a user interface perspective, it also means that graphical capabilities of the device are also improving, the interaction models are more advanced and require extra keys for navigation, and devices are becoming feature rich and inter-connected. From a hardware perspective, this transition also includes faster processors, more memory (built-in or expandable), built-in or attachable cameras, video conferencing capability, and Bluetooth. Many service providers are requiring their 3G devices to have larger and color screens, and support for Java or other application environments such as Brew. The addition of faster processors enables animations and transition effects. With camera capabilities, multimedia messaging is expected to be a key feature. When designing native applications, it is important to keep the device characteristics in mind and to understand the interaction model. That is, it's important to know the following:

- Which keys are mapped to specific actions
- If there is a navigation metaphor
- If there is a visual metaphor
- If there are specific screen elements and how are they used
- How text input works

This is necessary because users often grow attached to and become comfortable with the brand and interaction model of the device. They develop a mental model of how the device works and apply that to all applications. However, there may be times when an application must stray from the core interaction model. This occurs when the application cannot function with the keys provided on the device. For example, a game that requires a character to move in all four directions may easily be mapped to four-way scroll keys. But for a device with only a two-way scroll key, the key mapping for the character movement may have to be on the 2, 4, 6, and 8 keys in order for the game to be played, even though the device may not support that natively.

1.6.2   Interaction Models

Interaction models can differ between devices and are largely related to the physical keys available. For example, some devices may have a single programmable key or softkey dedicated to selecting or displaying menu options. Others may have two programmable keys or softkeys, one for selection and the other for displaying menu options. There are two significantly different interaction models here: one that relies on forward and back navigation, and a second that works from the notion of primary and secondary actions. There may also be dedicated actions for other keys, such as Send/End and numeric keys, depending on the application.

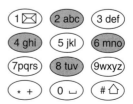

Figure 1.4   Standard keypad layout

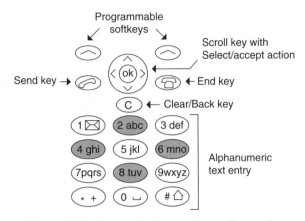

Figure 1.5   Example keypad configuration

1.6.3   Selection

The screen elements a device supports may also affect how an application is designed. For example, it is important to note the different methods for supporting single selection (selection for activation vs. selection for setting a variable), multiple selection (check boxes), and form-based input fields. Input methods for devices can also determine how an application can be written because some allow only a single input per screen (wizard input method) and others allow multiple inputs per screen. It is important to try to use similar or the same methods used by the device. Most often, the user interface is optimized for the devices: keypad, graphics, and applications.

For example, native applications designed by the device manufacturer may take advantage of the entire screen real estate, or that allotted by the user interface style. This includes the option of using status indicators, showing/hiding scroll indicators and/or scroll bars, and total control over the softkey and/or title areas. When designing downloadable applications, the device may have control over certain screen elements (e.g., status indicators, scroll bars, title, and softkey areas) and leave only a portion of the screen available. The content developer may have little control over what displays in those areas. Files that are not applications that can be downloaded (such as images, videos, MMS templates), may need to be designed specifically for a device and/or the capabilities of the application running and displaying that content.

1.6.4   Device Interaction Models

The examples below show the same application on three devices with various keys. Each interaction model demonstrates the same capabilities (e.g., the same feature), but the user can access the functions differently.

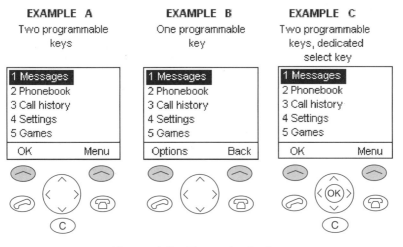

Figure 1.6   Example devices

Many device manufacturers map a shortcut to quickly exit an application and return to the idle screen. Depending on the device, this is often a single press or a press–hold of the End key (while not on a call) to execute a quick return to the idle screen. The End key may also be used to power the device on or off. Additionally, a few devices map the End key to a back function and allow the user to perform a save and back/exit action. The Send key is usually mapped only to the call creation or answer call function, unless it is shared as a softkey or options key.

1.6.5   Scrolling

There are four main types of scroll keys including (four-way, two-way, and jog-dial). Four-way scrolling devices can consist of a four-way rocker or joystick (with or without a navikey function; that is, a press-down function as described in Table 1.4, Example C). The two-way scroll key is generally a rocker, and some devices may also use volume keys for scrolling. A few devices use a jog dial, a rolling dial for up/down scrolling (or left/right scrolling within text). These come in two configurations: two-way, and two-way with selection.

1.6.6   Text Input Methods

The text input method is key to driving the interaction model. It is often dictated by the keys available on the device, or lack thereof, and relates to how text modes are selected, what characters can be entered, and how text fields (size and formatting), cursor movement, character deletion, and insertion are handled. Navigation into, out of, and between text fields is also significant.

There are a variety of ways the device manufacturer can designate input modes. They may assign all modes to one key, or provide input modes (alpha

Table 1.4   Example device interaction models

Example	Difference in interaction model
Example A	Primary option (OK) is on the primary key/softkey, other options are on a menu key/softkey (Menu); back and text deletion is on a clear (C) key.
Example B	All options are on the primary key/softkey; backward navigation and/or text deletion are on a second key/softkey.
Example C	A dedicated selection key between the scroll keys allows the user to select a screen element, such as a menu item, text input field, radio button, or check box. Primary option (OK) is on the primary key/softkey, other options are the second key/softkey (Menu); back and text deletion is on a clear (C) key.

Table 1.5   Scroll key interaction models

Scroll key	Example diagram	Interaction models
Four-way scroll		*Interaction 1:* Up and down scrolling is used for scrolling up and down menu lists. Left and right scroll keys are used for scrolling up and down the menu/tree hierarchy. *Interaction 2:* Up and down scrolling is used for scrolling up and down menu lists. User may scroll table cells up/down and left/right (e.g., in a calendar).
Two-way scroll		Up and down scrolling is used for scrolling up and down menu lists.
Jog dial		Up and down scrolling is used for scrolling menu lists. The device may/may not have additional scroll keys, if jog dial is located on the side of the handset.
Four-way jog dial		As described above; however, selection can be made via a push or pull mechanism of the dial to activate a menu and/or select an item. Handset may/may not have additional scroll key.

Table 1.6   Changing text mode interaction models

Input mode selection	Example diagram	Interaction models
Menu key	(Menu)	A designated menu key whereby the user can access various input modes. The menu may display on a new screen or as a pop-up menu.
Mode softkey	Softkey	The ability to change input modes may be accessed from a mode softkey. In this case, the device is likely to have two softkeys, one designated to changing the modes when the user is in a text input field/ query. The menu may display on a menu in a new screen, as a pop-up menu, or toggle the modes.
* or # key	* or #	The user may change the mode from either the *, #, or a combination. The modes may display on a menu in a new screen, as a pop-up menu, or toggle the modes.

characters vs. numbers vs. symbols vs. special text entry methods (e.g., T9) across a number of keys. In addition, there may be devices that display an input area, and upon selection a new screen or window is opened that permits text input.

1.7   User Interface Elements

There are factors other than interaction models that can also cause visual and inter-action differences between devices and affect the look and feel of an application.
These variables can include:

- Title bar
- Status indicators
- Use of icons
- Rendering menu lists
- Accelerators
- Menu scrolling
- Scroll bars
- Selection indication
- Localization of texts
- Custom or "smart" handling of input methods

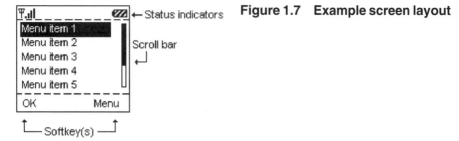

Figure 1.7   Example screen layout

Table 1.7   Numeric mode interaction models

Numeric mode selection	Example diagram	Interaction models
Menu key	Menu	The user may select numeric mode via a menu key. This may be in addition to the alpha modes.
Mode softkey	Softkey	The user selects numeric mode via a mode softkey. This may be in addition to alpha modes.
* or #	* or # key	The user selects numeric mode on the * or # key. This may be in addition to alpha modes, although it could be on the alternate key (e.g., shift is on * key and number mode on # key) or a press-hold of the alpha mode key.
0–9	0–9 keys	Interaction 1: Most devices allow the user to enter a number after cycling through the characters associated with the key (e.g., 2 key – a b c 2). Interaction 2: Some devices allow a press-hold to insert a number directly, sometimes in addition to a designated mode mentioned in Interaction 1.

Table 1.8   Symbols mode interaction models

Symbols selection	Example diagram	Interaction models
Menu key	Menu	The user selects a symbol screen via the menu key, which may be in addition to selecting other modes.
Mode softkey	Softkey	The user selects a symbols mode via a mode softkey. This may be in addition to alpha modes.
* or #	* or # key	The user selects symbols individually or via a symbols screen with either key or both keys.
1	1 key	Most devices allow access to a limited set of frequently used symbols from the 1 key. The symbols may differ depending on the application.

Table 1.9   Adding a space

Space key	Example diagram	Interaction models
1	1 key	The user may insert a space from the 1 key and may be in conjunction with another method mentioned below.
0	0 key	The user selects a space from the 0 key.
4-way scroll		**Interaction 1:** The user scrolls characters left and right with the scroll keys and inserts a space from the right scroll key when the cursor is at the end of the last character in the input field. **Interaction 2:** The user scrolls characters left and right with the up/down scroll keys and *only* allow a space to be entered with the right scroll key. In this case, the user may not scroll back to insert a space within previously entered text.
#	# key	Some devices map left and right scrolling within text on the * and # keys. In this case, some devices allow users to add a space at the end of the last character, which prohibits scrolling back to insert a space within previously entered text.

Title bar – A title bar is used to inform the users where they are in the menu hierarchy, the active application, or instructions. For devices that display a title, the text may do some or all of the following:

- Be fixed to display only the application name
- Provide instructions to the user (e.g., "Select your favorite")
- Be limited in width
- Scroll
- Be static
- Automatically truncate with or without ellipsis (. . .)
- May scroll more than one line

Status indicators – Indicators are used for displaying phone status (e.g., in-call, network connection, battery strength, in numeric mode, in smart input mode, in a data call, etc.). The display for status indicators varies between devices. A few devices still have an etched status indicator window, thereby limiting the notion of "new" indicators. Most devices have a "soft" indicator area, a region on the graphical display reserved for indicators, and can create and display items that are application specific. However, due to screen limitations, device manufacturers must set priorities, because not all relevant indicators can display at once.

Icons – Some devices display icons in menu lists or associate an application with an icon.

Menu lists – The device manufacturer may allocate only a line, a part of the screen, or the entire screen for displaying an item and/or an associated icon. Some devices display numbers preceding the menu text.

Accelerators – Many devices allow the user to quickly access a menu item by pressing an accelerator key in the range of 0–9. Some manufacturers display the number associated with a menu item next to it, while others display it in a header or indicator area. Another method displays the entire accelerator navigation path (e.g., 1-3-2-4) in a title or indicator area.

Menu scrolling – There are a variety of ways that devices can support menu scrolling depending on the type of menu (list vs. grid) and may be specific to a particular level within the menu hierarchy. Within a list, many devices support wrap-around scrolling. That is, scrolling up from the first item will display the last item in the list, and scrolling down from the last item will redisplay the first. It is important to note what type of menu can be used for various applications since it may not be appropriate to use a specific menu in certain conditions.

Scroll indicators – Many devices display scrolling indicators, and they vary in style. For example, a tab indicator (which can display on the top of a menu or on the right or left portion of the screen), scroll bar, or arrows at the top or bottom can indicate there are more items to scroll.

Selection indication – Most devices indicate selection by highlighting the text with reverse video or color.

Text localization – Device manufacturers can optimize the text for local applications to best fit the screen size. However, for downloadable or browser applications, it is important to be aware of lengthy texts. Texts that do not fit on one line may automatically wrap, scroll (character-by-character or word-by-word), or be

Figure 1.8 Sony Ericsson T61G showing tabs at the menu top level

truncated. Texts that are truncated may lose meaning and decrease application usability.

Custom input methods – Many devices support T9, Zi, or other "smart" input methods. In some cases, the input editor may allow direct input in the smart input mode. In other cases, due to language restrictions or software integration, the input editor may display in a new screen when selected.

1.8   When and What to Use (Markup, Native OS, or Messaging)

1.8.1   Case Study: Games, Information Applications, Messaging Applications

As discussed, there are many different ways to deliver an application to a device depending on the type of application, targeted user, and device capabilities. Deciding when and where to build an application based on a native operating system, browser based markup, or messaging heavily depends on the goals and purpose of the application and the types of content to be delivered.

Games
The gaming experience on mobile devices is clearly still evolving. High end phones with speedy processors, large available memory, and large displays have the potential to provide a platform equal to that of dedicated gaming devices. Phones will likely continue to be limited to the physical constraints of their primary function. As new phone platforms emerge, the majority of them are not likely to have joysticks or action buttons specifically tailored to game playing. Lower end, mass-market devices will continue to benefit from features that sediment down to the commodity level over time, and present even richer environments for gaming.

There are several classes of games, from action games that require rapid responses from the user and from the device, to strategic games like chess or Othello, to casino or card games, to board games such as Monopoly™, to role-playing games such as the classic adventure or dungeons and dragons. Any of these games could be played as a single player vs. device or in a head-to-head or even multiplayer mode. The table below presents some of the pros and cons for developing different types of games running in either a network or local environment.

Action based games such as Asteroids provide a much more sophisticated and meaningful user experience if architected to run in a local application environment. The local nature of the application allows for "fast twitch" type responses that are simply not possible to accomplish over a network. Graphics performance can be optimized by redrawing only the portions of the screen that require updating, and every key press event can be captured and bound to an action. Furthermore, when the user exits the application, the game can stay in a paused state, and be resumed exactly at the point of suspension.

The application may also interact with the browser and/or messaging applications in the handset. Even if the game does not require network access to operate, network resources could be used to provide new levels of play, upload high scores, provide "help" files, chat, and track usage and adoption. If the application is to be targeted at a variety of different devices, and the resources are available, the only way to ensure near universal availability is to develop discrete executable versions of the game for every targeted device.

On the other hand, an application that does not require constant or rapid interaction from the end user may be more elegantly architected to run within the context of a browser. Consider a strategy game such as chess, or even bridge. The results of each round of action in the game are not dependent upon how quickly decisions are made, but more on the long-term impact of these decisions. In these cases, network latency is perfectly acceptable, and a game played wholly within the context of the browser on a device may not only be feasible, but desirable, from the standpoint of both the user and the application developer.

Information Applications

The vast majority of the content available on the wired Web today can be categorized as "information applications." These include sports and news updates, which not only provide scores, standings, and news, but also real-time updates from games in progress; financial applications that provide real-time streaming data, the ability to execute transactions and review details; lookup applications such as yellow pages or corporate phone book services; and mapping services. Again, any of these could be provided on a mobile device via either an application that executes directly on the handset or from within the context of a browser. By designing an information application to run within a browser, the developer/designer can focus on the content being delivered rather than the network connections and required navigation constructs. User interaction is limited to simple query input, and forward/backward type navigation, but based on the information available, this is all that may be necessary. The integration of asynchronous push technology in the browsing environment allows update delivery, and fresh content can be presented even when the user is not actively engaged in the application, which is not something than can be accomplished in an application designed to run completely locally. While the layout of content within the application is constrained by the rendering capabilities/limitations

Type of game	Description	Local/native	Network based
Action	Example: Motor cross racing, bowling, golf	Best if the application requires heavy graphics and/or is intensive on the device's processor. Must be built for the specific device capabilities, taking into consideration multimedia support on a given device.	Can be used for less intensive graphic graphic games (e.g., golf) where the a result can come from a database or quick calculation. Good for devices that do not support downloading or running applications on the device OS.
Board/card games	Example: Checkers or chess	Best if the application is designed as a player vs. device game. Also, a richer graphical experience can be provided as the entire screen, or areas can be repainted at will.	If the game is simple, can be used for head-to-head play, or tournaments. Graphics for the game must be delivered as a single file, or potentially images within table cells.
Role playing/fantasy	Example: Dundgeons and Dragons	Best if the application is graphics intensive. Can also be used to create a MUD if network access is permitted by user and/or network.	Can be used to provide a text based, or lightweight graphics experience. If there are constrained choices that can be made at each turn, can provide easy access to a wide variety of clients.

Table 1.10   Environment to use when designing games

Type of application	Description	Local/native	Network based
Sports/news	Provide up-to-the-minute information, stories, and images	Can provide a streaming "gamecast" type experience with play-by-play information updates without user intervention. Requires network connection as well as significant interface design.	Low overhead to get information quickly to user. Asynchronous notifications can be pushed to alert user to updated information. Limited in ability to provide "live" interaction.
Financial	Stock market information services	Can provide a live, streaming ticker or moving graphs that update transaction by transaction. Requires constant network interaction for data feeds, not possible to deliver information when the application is not active.	Information can be pushed to the user asynchronously based on predefined triggers. Simple, transaction based interactions are very simple to build.
Lookup services	Yellow pages, corporate directories	Can be accessed at any time, regardless of network availability. Can be tightly integrated into phone functions of the device. Can leverage location information available in some devices.	Single data store for information, so no synchronization issues. Can leverage location based services from the service provider.
Mapping	Current location, driving directions	Can provide richer interactions with data via zooming and panning without network connections. Current location can only be gained from a GPS-enabled device or end user input.	Can leverage location based services from service provider.

Table 1.11   Environment to use when designing information applications

of the browser environment, this will not impose undue limitations for a sports update application.

A live broadcast of a baseball game can be built most successfully by using a native/local application rather than from within the context of the browser. This sort of application could be architected in a client/server model wherein a native application running on a handset could register with a network server and listen for events. If a device has sufficient screen real estate, the display could be partitioned with an area delivering the color commentary along with the statistics of the ongoing action. While the same raw data could be delivered via a browser, updates would have to be manually initiated by the end user. When a client-side scripting language such as ECMAScript becomes available on mobile devices, it may become possible to provide a much richer experience within the context of the browser.

A corporate phone directory may be most effectively delivered via a browser interface. If an internal directory is already available online via light-weight directory access protocol (LDAP) or even with an HTML interface to a database, this information is very simply ported to a wireless device. There would be no need to engineer a navigation structure or network connection, and numbers could be dialed directly from within the browser by using the wtai:// directive from WML or the tel: directive from XHTML.

Messaging Applications

Even as devices continue to become more powerful and sophisticated, simple messaging applications will continue to remain an important part of every device. Messaging itself can be viewed as a collection of applications and interfaces. At the lowest level is SMS, which forms the foundation for just about every messaging service due to its simplicity and near universal prevalence. Nearly every other messaging application or service relies on SMS for delivery of some sort. These other applications include MMS, Instant Messaging, WAP Push, and chat rooms.

The decision to build a network based or local messaging application hinges on whether the messages are expected to be received asynchronously, even when the application itself is not currently active. Unless the application has nearly complete access to system resources on the device, the only way to receive asynchronous messages is by to build a messaging application that runs either entirely over SMS, is based on MMS, or runs within a browser in conjunction with WAP Push. If the messaging application can function within a synchronous environment, such as a chat room or instant messaging, the application can be built to run as a local client or run within the context of the browser. By building these types of applications within a browser, XHTML and CSS can be leveraged to create background environments for chats that can be changed on the fly with no engineering work needed on the client side.

1.9 Tips

The following high-level tips apply to device properties and are important to be aware of when designing applications.

	Description	Problems	Possible resolutions
Using color	The quality of mobile phone LCD screens is not as good as those on a PC, and while they continue to improve, color balance and saturation is very variable between screen suppliers.	Subtle shading and some tones (especially in the yellow range) will tend to wash out, and care should be taken to test images on representative devices before deploying. The bit depth available may be 4, 8, or 16 bits for color, and 2 or 4 for black and white and grayscale.	Refer to the specification sheet from the device manufacturer developer Web site for more information.
Using sound	Social and cultural etiquette may dictate whether it is acceptable for sounds to play, and depending on the situation, it is imperative that users be able to easily turn sound on and off at the device and application level, and also within the application.	Some devices do not offer independent volume keys. For these devices, the user may only adjust the volume from a settings menu, while the phone is ringing, or while in a voice call.	Some applications should allow the user to control sound volume and whether it is turned on/off. For example, in a messaging application, a user may want to control whether sounds play within a message, or if there are several sounds attached, which should play and when.
Fonts	Some devices support various font sizes, styles, and character sets, but there is no standard across devices.	Using font styles other than Normal may cause the device to render text that is difficult to read. Not all font sets are provided in a device. Know what languages and character sets are supported.	Do not rely on use of font styles or sizes. Refer to the specification sheet from the device manufacturer's developer Web site for more information.

Table 1.12   Tips for designing mobile applications

Screen size	Screen sizes differ between devices. Also, screen size is not an indicator of pixels per inch. Not all devices have square pixels. Pixel height/width ratio differs between manufacturers.	An application or image designed for a given device may look small or be cropped on another device. An image on one device may look stretched if pixels are rectangular.	Test the application and/or images on various devices. Refer to the device manufacturer's developer Web site for screen size information, or examine the screen with a magnifying loupe.
Key mapping	Devices differ with respect to the number and meaning of the keys.	Not all devices have the same keys or use keys in the same way.	Know what keys are available on the device and what is the interaction model for a given device. Tailor the application to match as closely as possible to the interaction model of the device.
File formats	There are no standard image, sound, or media formats for mobile devices.	Not all devices support the same file formats. Thus, a sound created for one device may not work on another.	Test the file on various devices. Refer to the device manufacturer's developer Web site for support file types.
Memory	Devices are often made for target user groups; thus, the amount of available memory can differ between devices.	Applications that are too large or require too much processor memory may fail to run or may not be able to be downloaded.	Test the application on target devices to ensure the application can be downloaded and run on the given device. Refer to the device manufacturer's developer Web site for available memory and memory constraints.

	Description	Problems	Possible resolutions
Input fields	Devices support input methods in various ways. Some support inline editing, some require the user to select the field and access a new screen, and others only allow one input field per screen. Smart input modes can interfere in some applications.	Formatted text fields that open to a new screen may not allow auto-fill or lose essential information. For example, date text fields that require the user to enter dates with a particular format (e.g., mm/dd/yyyy) may cause problems if the user is not properly informed of the format or cannot easily enter the format. Some formatted fields require localization; e.g., mm/dd/yyyy is correct for North America, but should be reformatted for Europe and Asia. Text input fields requiring names, addresses, or passwords may cause problems for smart input methods.	Take care when using formatted text fields. Avoid when possible. Be sure to provide localization as necessary. For native applications that are provisioned in the factory, the device manufacturer should auto-format the field, when necessary. Set the default state to Off for an input field requiring names, addresses, or passwords. Allow fields to be case insensitive.
Refreshing the data	Time sensitive applications require refreshing the screen with the new information (for example, sports scores, and traffic maps).	Applications that require updating the information are ineffective if the information is not updated or cannot easily be refreshed.	Allow the application to auto-refresh or allow the user to refresh/reload the data.

Table 1.12 *Continued*

1.10 Outtakes from Usability Testing

In general, when designing new products and features, get to know the customer. At the beginning of the project, survey existing users about how they use the product today, their likes, dislikes, expectations, and suggestions for new features, and use the data when setting product requirements. Then test the product in the design phase with a similar subject pool to see if the design answers requirements.

Here are some high-level findings from many usability tests and user surveys of data services and applications.

1.10.1 Issue: Navigation

Users report that they hate having to navigate down deep through hierarchical menus to find what they're looking for. For example, a link to soccer scores buried three or four screens down is tedious to access and may color the user's perception of data services.

Impact
In some cases, this was why users stopped using the mobile Web. Users were frustrated by having to follow long navigational paths each time, and by the cost of connection.

Recommendation
Allow users quick access to frequently used locations. At least allow an easy way to bookmark, and keep links at the top level (of the phone or browser). Think about offering push updates to data that users access frequently. Allow the user to set a priority level and provide alerts if the data meets their criteria of high priority. For example, in an application that enables tracking travel conditions, alert the user if a flight is delayed or cancelled, or if road conditions change.

1.10.2 Issue: Cost

Cost is a driving factor for use. Many consumers (especially in younger age groups) will not become users of services that they perceive as unduly expensive. For example, while the cost of sending SMS is considered negligible, users avoid sending messages to multiple recipients if they incur a cost per address.

Impact
Users will find ways to work around this, such as forwarding messages in a chain, or avoid sending messages to many recipients. This causes problems because friends sometimes don't get messages, due to network latency or a break in the chain.

Recommendation
Work with and share usability data with those who can solve the problem: in this case, the service provider. From a UI perspective, this problem can be avoided by allowing users to combine several names into a group address, with a flat charge.

However, until the service provider modifies the billing model, this problem may continue to exist.

1.10.3   Issue: Login and Password

On the desktop, users often have problems when being required to log on to a site and create a user name and password. The user name they create may be rejected, and they may accept one generated for them by the site. If not prompted to keep a record, users forget the name on subsequent visits. Sometimes this user name becomes their persona, and they may not realize they accepted "Aj326B7o" as their email address, or know how to change it later. Passwords have similar issues. On mobile devices, these issues are magnified by the difficulty in entering text and changing text modes.

Consider the following:

- Is it necessary for the user to log in each time?
- Does this password need to match a desktop Web interface?
- Supply a confirmation dialog and email (if available) upon registration.
- Allow changing and saving the data.

Because text entry is difficult on a mobile phone, give additional consideration to:

- Can the login be the mobile number or device ID?
- Can the password be numeric only for easier text entry (as in a PIN)?
- Can the login and password be case insensitive to avoid multiple mode changes?

1.10.4   Issue: Localization of Terms and Abbreviations

Users are sometimes confused by terms that are not current in their location. For example, British users were unable to complete a task to find the closest cash access point at a bank because they were not familiar with the term ATM (Automated Teller Machine). They expected to see cashpoint or cash machine in this context. The site was designed in the US, but had not been localized.

1.10.5   Issue: Help

Provide users with help or other information, but do not force it upon them. Provide a menu option, a timeout that goes to help, and/or provide a link on a splash screen for a game.

1.11   References

1.11.1   Industry

GSM   http://www.gsmworld.com
M-Services   http://www.gsmworld.com/technology/services/index.shtml

CDMA	http://www.cdg.org/index.asp
	http://www.emc-database.com

1.11.2   Market Research

Yankee Group	http://www.yankeegroup.com
ICM	http://www.icmresearch.co.uk/default.htm
EMC	http://www.emc-database.com/

1.11.3   ISP

Openwave	http://developer.openwave.com
Nokia	http://forum.nokia.com

1.11.4   Service Providers

Vodaphone	http://via.vodafone.com
Sprint	http://developer.sprintpcs.com
Telstra	http://www.telstra.com.au/mobile

1.11.5   Operator Requirements Documents

GSM	Worldhttp://www.gsmworld.com/technology/applications/index.shtml
Sprint	http://developer.sprintpcs.com

1.11.6   Environments

Symbian	http://www.symbian.com/developer/tools.html
Java	http://java.sun.com
	http://developer.java.sun.com/servlet/SessionServlet?url=/developer/
Brew	http://www.qualcomm.com/brew

1.11.7   Device Manufacturers

Nokia	http://forum.nokia.com
Ericsson	http://www.ericsson.com/mobilityworld
Siemens	http://www2.siemens.fi/developers.jsp?cid=devgar
Sharp	http://www.sharp-mobile.com/index.asp
Samsung	http://www.samsungelectronics.com/mobile_phone/index.asp

Chapter 2

Designing Voice Applications

Jennifer Balogh, Nicole Leduc

2.1 Introduction

Cell phones have introduced us to a world where mobility coexists with communication. Combine the mobility of the cell phone with speech recognition technology, and we now have a revolutionary way to access information and conduct business by interacting with computers, anytime, anywhere. What's more, mobile callers can get to information without extra equipment such as wireless modems, WAP phones, or Palm Pilots; all they need is a simple phone. Speech-enabled services offer the added benefit of gathering and presenting information all in the auditory modality. So when driving or on the go, callers can attend to their environment without having to look at a screen or press buttons. Voice user interfaces (VUIs) are not without their challenges, though. Audio is transient and cognitively demanding. In addition, callers have high expectations of the technology's capabilities and assume that any utterance of theirs should be recognized by the system.

This chapter will provide an overview of speech technologies including speech recognition, verification, and text-to-speech. We describe the basic components of a VUI: the system messages, grammars, and application logic, and discuss these in the context of the underlying technology. We then step through a tried and tested design and development process. Unlike other software development tasks, the design of a speech application requires the added sensibility to the human-computer dialog and the need for error recovery behavior that accommodates the less-than-one-hundred-percent accuracy of speech recognition. Because of this, the design and development process relies on phases unique to a VUI including the selection of the right voice for the system, the crafting of sample dialogs, and the tuning of the recognition performance. We present two case studies of successful speech application deployments targeted for mobile callers. Finally, from these studies, we extract basic guidelines of how to design an effective user interface.

In the worlds of science fiction, people to talk to computers: *2001* introduced us to Hal, *Star Trek* brought us the Halodeck, and *Star Wars*, C3PO. As modern technologies continue to advance, the worlds of science fiction become closer and closer to our own experiences today. Now, it is not unusual to pick up a phone and start talking to a computer to get flight arrival times or to check the balance of a credit card. Some automated systems like Claire, sprint's virtual customer care agent, are starting to take on their own personalities, just like the artificial intelligence of the movies.

2.1.1   Some Background on Speech Technology

Even though speech recognition is only now becoming commonplace, it has been with us for several decades, and in that time has appeared in many forms. "Radio Rex," a children's toy in the 1920's, was the first success story in the field of speech recognition. Inside the toy, a magnet held a dog inside its dog house. When the dog's name was called, the energy in the vowel sound for "Rex" broke an electrical circuit and a spring pushed the dog out of the house. Many years later, speech technology moved from the toy industry to computers. Apple sold a model that could understand simple desktop commands, such as opening and closing applications. The computer would be christened with a name, and every time the user wanted to tell the computer a command, the user would say this name before the command. Speech recognition in this capacity was seen mostly as a novelty and never quite replaced the mouse. However, there were other attempts at ridding the user of the keyboard and mouse with dictation software. Dictation allows the user to sit in front of a computer and dictate a letter without ever resting a finger on the keyboard. Since the user chooses what to dictate, the range of possible utterances that the system has to recognize is limitless. The challenge for technology is not only the recognition of continuous speech, but speech that is unconstrained in content. To overcome these obstacles, the software requires an individual to train the acoustic models with his or her voice by reading designated passages. Similar to dictation, speech recognition is also being used for transcription. In order to automatically catalog information (for example, in news broadcasts), the system not only has to extract words from an acoustic stream, but it has to identify the general content of the speech as well. Here, speech recognition is combined with natural language understanding to reconstruct both the form and meaning of the incoming speech. Now, children's toys are (again) becoming more technologically savvy with speech recognition.

Looking at most of these systems, it seems that speech recognition is a technology to be enjoyed while sitting in front of the computer (or in the kids' playroom). But a second look takes us to one of the most quickly evolving domains for speech recognition – the mobile context where people can pick up a phone from anywhere in the world and talk to an automated system to get information or make a transaction. A huge benefit of automated speech applications over the phone is that they truly are accessible from anywhere. No desktop machines, laptops, PDAs, or other special devices are needed; any ordinary phone will do (even a rotary).

Given the cost savings of automating call centers and the convenience of using the phone, many call centers have already made heavy use of touch tone systems, but the additional enhancements of speech from the users' perspective are influencing companies to move over to speech. Some deployed speech systems include American Airline's flight information system, Sears's call router, UPS's package tracking system, Sprint's "Claire", TellMe and BeVocal's voice portals, and Yahoo's Yahoo! by Phone. With more and more systems becoming publicly available, the question arises as to how satisfied are end users with these speech solutions and how does speech compare with alternative services such as touch tone systems, the Web, and human agents. A benchmark survey conducted in 1999 and 2000 suggests that users are satisfied with automated speech systems (LeDuc et al., 2001).

2.1.2   Caller Satisfaction with Speech Systems

The results of Leduc et al.'s benchmark study show that 87 percent of participants in the 2000 survey were satisfied with speech systems compared to 83 percent in 1999, showing that the technology is becoming more and more accepted. Some benefits of speech from the users' perspectives, as discovered from debriefing interviews, are that callers no longer have to take the phone from their ears and fumble around the keypad. Speech also introduces a pronounced benefit for callers on the go who do not have the time or equipment to log in to a computer. Those who accessed the system on a mobile phone, especially in the car, were most satisfied. Users cited speed, efficiency, and ease of use as reasons why they were satisfied with speech. When compared to human agents, touch tone systems and the Web, 75 percent of the users in the 1999 survey said that speech was the same or better than the method they were using before. In 2000, this percentage rose to 82 percent. Users think speech is better than agents because they do not have to wait on hold and can access the system 24/7. Previous Web users mentioned mobility as the reason they prefer speech. Overall, the surveys suggest that speech recognition provides an incredibly powerful and intuitive interface for humans to communicate with computers. So why has the technology taken so long to mature?

2.1.3   How Speech Recognition Works

Speech recognition only started making a splash in the 80s and 90s because of the increased computational power and advances in digital signal processing. Even now, recognition engines do not perform at 100 percent, although accuracy continues to increase. It is a difficult problem with many components at work. First, models of the acoustics, phonetics, and grammar of a particular language have to be built, and then the engine has to use these models on the speech of an individual speaker to understand what he or she said.

To build an acoustic model for continuous speech recognition, millions and millions of utterances are collected from different speakers. The speech is divided into *triphones* that make up the sounds of any given word. Conceptually, the sounds that make up words are thought of as phonemes. For instance, the word *sport* is made up of five phonemes: /s/, /p/, /o/, /r/, and /t/; whereas the word *short* is made up of four since /sh/ is one sound (represented by two letters). Now a single phoneme sounds very different when in the context of other phonemes. In English for example, when /p/ begins a word it is aspirated, making the /p/ in *port* sound very different from the /p/ in *sport*. Because of these context effects, each phoneme is more precisely classified based on the sounds that surround it. The different contexts for /p/ are captured in different triphones where /p/ is the middle sound. The triphone [spo] is used in the word *sport*; whereas the triphone [#po], where # means the beginning of a word, is used in *port*. Once there is a sufficient amount of recorded data for each triphone, the recordings are used to train an *acoustic model* of the sounds of a language.

Speech recognition also requires a *dictionary*. The dictionary contains a written representation of the phonemes that speakers typically use to say all the common words in a language. For some words there is more than one entry because different sounds are used in different dialects. For example, some people pronounce *fire* as one syllable and others pronounce it as two. The difference in pronunciations result in two entries in the dictionary: *f aj *r* and *f aj r* (where *aj* is the sound in *side* and **r* is the sound in *bird*). Entries can be added for words not contained in the general dictionary such as technical jargon and proper names; entries can also be added for uncommon pronunciations for words already in the dictionary.

In addition to a model of the sounds of the language and a dictionary that defines what sounds make up words, there is a finite-state *grammar* that models the words, phrases, and sentences that callers are expected to say at every point during the dialog. For most commercial speech systems, grammars are defined exhaustively by a grammar developer. For some engines, the semantic content of the word strings is also defined in the grammar. Then, the acoustic model, dictionary, and grammar are all compiled together to create a *node array* of all the expected sequences of sounds (which in turn make words, phrases, and sentences).

Another approach to grammar representation is a *statistical language model* (SLM) and a *natural language understanding* (NLU) component. SLMs are not written manually, but are trained from actual user utterances, and thus are best for unconstrained responses to the system that are difficult for a human grammar developer to predict (for example, when responding to an open prompt such as "How can I help you?") The SLM encapsulates the probabilities that some words follow other words in the dialog. This data-driven approach requires the models to be trained on hundreds of thousands of caller utterances. Because the SLM will be used in a specific context, the model must be trained on utterances from the same context. The SLM takes the utterance as input and produces the string of words that were most likely said. A separate natural language understanding (NLU) component assigns meaning to the string of words. This is done in many different ways. Some systems use a lexicon that defines parts of speech for each word. Then a series of rules defines which parts of speech make up phrases. For example, a noun phrase can consist of an adjective and a noun. Finally, the semantics for the critical pieces of information are encoded. Other systems embed the NLU into a node array. Once models of the probabilities and rules of the sounds, words, syntax, and semantics are in place for a given language, then these models are used to not only understand the words the person said, but to attach meaning to the utterance.

When a caller picks up the phone and starts interacting with a speech system, the sound from the telephone line is picked up by the system. First, the acoustic signal undergoes some preprocessing to cancel out any echo introduced by the phone line. A special algorithm encapsulated in an *endpointer* is applied to the utterance in order to detect when the caller starts speaking. Often there are other sounds prevalent in the caller's environment such as car doors slamming and static on the line, ideally, these external sounds should be ignored, leaving only the caller's speech to be analyzed by the system. Once speech has been detected, the audio data are sent to the *front-end*, which segments the speech into small frames of about 10 milliseconds, with 80 samples per frame. The characteristics of the sound across various frequencies are extracted and digitized. All the processing that takes place after this point is done on the digitized sample and not the original audio.

The speech recognizer then takes this digitized sample and produces a textual representation of the speech. The recognizer does this by searching for the best path through the node array to determine which triphone has been spoken as well as determining which word and phrase it is a part of. Since the number of possibilities is extremely large, the search space is pruned by eliminating very unlikely paths based on a computed likelihood score. The engine generates a set of possible hypotheses of what the utterance might be and the semantic content of the most likely hypothesis is returned to the application. The decisions about how the application handles different recognition hypotheses and which prompts to play are all part of the voice user interface (VUI).

Speech recognition often works in concert with other speech technologies such as speaker verification and text-to-speech. Speaker verification identifies who an individual caller is by mapping the characteristics of their speech to a previously stored representation of their voice called a *voiceprint*. The caller "enrolls" in a system by providing some samples of his or her voice by saying random digit strings, for example, or repeating canned phrases. Once the caller has enrolled, the system simply has to gather a few samples of speech to match against the stored voiceprint. If the current voice matches, the caller is verified; otherwise, the system assumes an imposter is trying to pose as the user and the caller is transferred or rejected by the system. Voice authentication is the perfect alternative to requiring users to remember a myriad of passwords and PINs.

Text-to-speech (TTS) or synthesized speech allows the system to render dynamic text into speech. This is an important capability for systems that read unpredictable and dynamic information to the caller, such as email. Many words differ in pronunciation depending on their part of speech. For example, the following sentence has two instances of the word *content*: "I a.m content reading this magazine, even though it is void of any content." The first instance of content is an adjective and is pronounced with stress on the second syllable; whereas, the second instance is a noun and is pronounced with stress on the first. The engine needs to make a decision about how to pronounce each word. To do this, it tags each word according to its part of speech. Then, the individual words are looked up in a pronunciation dictionary, which contains information about which phonemes make up the word and how it should be stressed. Once the engine "knows" how to pronounce the word, it searches a database of small, prerecorded segments of audio files recorded by a human voice actor. The engine selects segments that best match the current word or phrase given its context and then concatenates the segments. The engine usually contains additional algorithms to blend the concatenated recordings and create an appropriate prosodic contour over the entire utterance. Even though most informants continue to prefer human recordings to TTS, the engines are becoming more natural-sounding and intelligible, and as such, are becoming more prevalent in speech systems. Because of the utility of both speaker verification and TTS, these technologies are often integrated into speech recognition systems to create an entire solution.

2.1.4 The Elements of a Voice User Interface

The elements of a VUI are prompts, grammars, and application logic. The prompts, or system messages, are all the recordings played to the user during the dialog; the grammars exhaustively define what the caller is expected to say in response to each prompt; and the application logic maps out the specific actions the application takes in response to the callers' utterances or other events such as database hits or system errors. As an example, the following is a sample dialog between a caller and flight information application:

System: Thank you for calling Are We There Jet Airlines. What's the departure city?
Caller: San Francisco, California.
System: And the arrival city?
Caller: Boston, Massachusetts.
System: Okay, now tell me the departure date.
Caller: December 21st.
System: And what's the departure time?
Caller: 9 a.m.
System: You want the flight from San Francisco, California to Boston, Massachusetts on Friday, December 21st at 9 a.m. Is that right?
Caller: Yes.

The welcome prompt is the first thing the caller hears after dialing into the system. The dialog design specifies the exact words that the system uses to greet the caller and ask for the departure city. The designer must also define the grammar, and the main responses to be covered in that grammar. After the initial prompt, the active grammar might include all the major US cities, some popular international cities, airport names, popular airport codes, and responses such as "I don't know". The semantics of what the caller said are returned to the application from the recognizer. In the dialog above, [<city san_francisco> <state ca> <airport sfo>] might have been returned. Since the departure city was provided, the application logic moves on to ask what the arrival city is. If the caller had said "New York," which is serviced by two airports, then the application logic would ask the caller which airport in New York. And the dialog would move on from there. Anything that the caller hears from the system and every utterance that the caller is expected to say in response are all a part of the voice user interface.

2.1.5   Design and Development of Speech Applications

Speech applications go through a similar process of design and development as other software products, but because speech exists only in the auditory modality, there are some additional phases of the project unique to speech such as voice talent selection, prompt recording, and recognition tests. There are also unique challenges that need to be addressed. First, as mentioned above, the accuracy of speech recognition is not 100 percent yet. As such, designers need to accommodate errors and also set user expectations of what the system can do. Commonly, callers mistake automated voice systems for real people, and they talk to the system as if it were a reasoning human being. Unfortunately, the callers' utterances are often long and unpredictable, so the recognizer rejects them, leaving the callers in a state of frustration.

Another challenge for speech is that the audio stream is ephemeral, and therefore very cognitively demanding. With a graphical user interface, information remains visible on the screen at all times. Users can never forget what option to select because the choices are clearly displayed on the screen. In the audio modality, the caller has to recall from memory what the commands are. Remembering what to say can be especially taxing if there are many choices offered in menus and if those choices are complex phrases. Since many speech specialists have already taken on these challenges, a learned process of design has been developed to help in the creation of effective, user-centered designs. There are five main steps in the process of designing and developing a speech application: Requirements Definition, High-Level Design, Detailed Design, Production, and Tuning and Validation.

2.2   Requirements Definition

The goal of the Requirements Definition phase is to understand the needs of three entities: the end user, the business deploying the system, and the application itself. Decisions made at the Requirements Definition stage will affect all other phases of the project, so a thorough definition is critical. The client is an important resource for information about the caller. Most already have touch tone systems in place, so designers of speech systems can take advantage of statistics from these legacy systems. The business will probably have profiled their customer base and may have a bounty of information about the customers' demographics and usage patterns. Talking directly to the customers also uncovers important information about how the users feel about the business, current services, and new technology. Understanding who the callers are and what motivates them can have a huge impact on the overall design. For example, the prompts played in a system for a conservative bank will be vastly different from those of a horoscope service. Design strategies for novice, one-time users will be different from those of expert users who call the system several times a day. All this information needs to be available to the designer who will use it in subsequent phases of the project.

Understanding the business is also a critical step in the Requirements Definition phase. In particular, four aspects about the business should be clearly identified: the business case; the corporate image and brand; other available services; and the rollout plan. When designing a speech application, the designer needs to understand the business case so that decisions will be made that are in synch with the perceived value of the service. The business might want to cut costs by increasing automation rates. Knowing this will help the designer focus on high task completion rates and efficiency as opposed to entertainment and audio landscapes. Corporate image and branding are also important because they will influence such things as the style of the persona and the actor chosen to be the voice of the service. Often when a user survey suggests that a particular voice talent is the preferred choice, the business will select a different voice talent that better matches their corporate image. If other services are available to customers, then the speech system needs to be able to gain access to the same information database. Knowledge about how the speech system will coordinate with representatives' hours, and how transfers to other touch tone systems will take place need to be included in the design. If there is a touch tone system already in place, the speech application should be designed with speech in mind, and not map directly onto the touch tone system's rigid menu structure. And finally, depending on the rollout plan, information about key commands and system functionality will need to be integrated into marketing materials. The knowledge obtained about the business, along with the customer information, will be fed into the high-level design and help establish the metrics for measuring application success.

The final step in the Requirements Definition step is to define the general functionality of the system. What information will callers access and what major tasks will callers be able to perform? The designer and implementer need to consider account formats, PINs, information needed for database hits, news feeds, potential areas of latency, and any other aspect in which data structures or logistics of the application may influence the VUI design.

Based on the information gathered so far including who the callers are, what the business motivations are, and what the functionality of the application will be, a formal requirements definition document is written. All the design decisions going forward will be grounded in this document. Then the project can move on to the next phase, High-Level Design.

2.3   High-Level Design

The goal of the High-Level Design phase is to create a framework for the detailed design that is based on the Requirements Definition. The first step is to define a consistent sound and feel of the application through metaphor, persona, and the audio environment. Once this framework is established, the designer can start to propose design strategies consistent with the needs of the end user, the business, and the capabilities of the technology.

In a VUI, metaphors are a tangible analogy for the abstract organizational scheme of an application. Research has shown that when callers are given a metaphor, they are better able to navigate a speech system and complete tasks (Dutton et al., 1999). A metaphor can be as simple as representing the type of human agent the caller would normally be talking to (for example, a broker for a brokerage call center). It can represent the way callers will perceive information (for example, as if they were on a floor of a department store or looking at the page of a magazine).

For the most part, metaphors will be realized through prompt wording and nonverbal audio (NVA), including music clips and natural sounds. The following is an example of the same prompts from two different automated shopping systems that use different metaphors (taken from Dutton et al., 1999):

Department store metaphor

- "Which floor do you want?"
- "Going up! [sound effect: elevator moving] Floor five, clothing department."
- "Shirts are hanging up on your left, trousers are on the rail straight ahead of you, and jackets are over on your right."

Magazine metaphor

- "Which page would you like to turn to?"
- "Page five, clothing items [sound effect: pages turning]."
- "You've got shirts in the first picture, trousers in the second, and jackets in the third."

The metaphor is the overlying organizational scheme of the application, while the persona is the mental image of a personality or character that callers infer from the system. If using a "person" metaphor such as a broker, the persona is the characterization of the specific broker the user will be interacting with. The persona needs to embody the service and also appeal to the end user. It needs to reflect the corporate image of the business, while representing the callers' expectations and preferences in the aggregate. Research has shown that people generally enjoy talking to characters who are more similar to themselves than different (Reeves and Nass, 1996). Creating a chatty or extremely laid-back persona for a banking application in which callers will be managing money would be a misguided design decision given that most callers conducting banking transactions would rather interact with someone who is accurate, polite, and professional. Creating a persona is like developing a character for a short story or a movie. The details of the character should be anchored in a specific point of reference, such as a storyboard, that breathes life into the persona. This description will be a guide for those who are working with the detailed dialog design and call flow, and important to those crafting prompts and selecting and coaching the voice actor.

Closely tied to the metaphor and persona is the audio environment. Nonverbal audio (NVA) includes all non-speech sounds such as audio brands (heard upon entry into the system), background music, and sounds or music that covers latency. Within a single application, the NVA should be designed to have a consistent "sound and feel", with the same sound in the same role throughout the application.

Once the framework for the general sound and feel of the application has been developed, the designer begins creating sample dialogs and high-level call flows. The sample dialogs consist of preliminary system prompts interleaved with realistic responses from the caller. The sample dialogs give a flavor for how the system will sound and behave. The high-level call flow is simply a flow diagram of the call flow. Generally, detailed information such as error recovery and reentry prompts are left out of the flowcharts at this phase in the process. The idea is to capture the main functionality of the system graphically so that all parties agree on what is to be designed. The general structure that has been thought through in the High-Level Design phase will serve as the backbone for the more detailed design work in the next step of the process.

2.4 Detailed Design

In the Detailed Design phase, the designer fleshes out the sample dialogs and creates exhaustive call flows. The following is an example of a sample dialog that covers disambiguation, contextual inference, error recovery, and confirmation.

System: Thank you for calling Are We There Jet Airlines. What's the departure city?
Caller: San Francisco, California.
System: And the arrival city?
Caller: New York, New York
System: Is that New York Kennedy, New York La Guardia, or neither of these?
Caller: New York Kennedy.
System: Okay, now tell me the departure date.
Caller: Tomorrow.
System: And what's the departure time?
Caller: Uh . . .
System: Sorry, I didn't catch that. Just say an approximate departure time or tell me whether it's in the morning, afternoon, or evening.
Caller: Afternoon.
System: You want the flight from San Francisco, California to New York Kennedy on Tuesday November 5th at 1 p.m. Is that right?
Caller: Yes.

The VUI contains all the information about what prompts will greet the caller and the grammar of what the caller is expected to say. Some standard commands also need to be handled in the grammar (and every grammar in the application), including *help*, *repeat*, *operator*, *goodbye*, and *start over*. These are typically referred to as *universals* or *globals* since they are available to the caller at any time. The actions taken by the application after hearing any universal command needs to be designed into the dialog. For example, when the application thinks the caller has said "goodbye," does it play a goodbye message and end the call or does it go through a confirmation dialog to be sure the recognizer did not misunderstand the caller? Some standards committees such as the European Telecommunications Standard Institute (ETSI) are starting to develop standard universal commands and actions to encourage consistent terminology and behavior across applications. (For more information, see http://portal.etsi.org/tb/status/status.asp.)

Once the system has received a departure destination, it prompts the caller for the arrival city. If the caller had said, "New York, New York," as in the dialog above, the application would have to disambiguate the response, given that there are two airports for New York City. Sometimes the recognizer thinks the caller said something that the caller actually did not; these are often called *mis-recognitions* or *false accept*. If the caller were to encounter the disambiguation dialog because of a misrecognition, then the choices in the prompt would not make sense: neither New York, Kennedy nor New York, La Guardia would be appropriate if the caller had asked for New Port. Therefore, the disambiguation prompt includes "neither of these" to allow the caller to get out of the current dialog. It is critical in all speech applications that the grammar and prompts be co-ordinated. If, for example, the grammar did not cover "neither of these," then the caller's response would never be correctly recognized. The caller would come away extremely frustrated since compliance with the system prompts would ultimately lead to failure. Unfortunately, the problem of mismatched prompts and grammars is quite common, especially when prompts are modified during dialog tuning but grammars are left untouched. An important guideline for design is to make sure prompts and grammars are always coordinated.

Dialog designers always have to be aware of context. Sometimes they have to design the system so that it infers what the caller means. When callers are asked for the departure date, for example, they will think in terms of the current day. Therefore, the application needs to expect relative responses such as today, tomorrow, and this Sunday. The recognizer, of course, does not know what the current day is – it simply returns to the application what the caller said. The application must take the information and translate it into a specific date.

Another important element of a VUI is error behavior. The application has to deal with situations where callers stay quiet on the line, say things that are not expected, speak too much, and use touch tones when speech is expected. The recognizer returns each of these types of errors to the application, but it is up to the dialog designer to decide how the application should react. In the sample dialog above, the caller was not sure of the exact time of the flight and simply responded to the prompt with the conversational filler, "uh." Since this response was not explicitly covered in the grammar (often referred to as an *out of grammar (OOG)* utterance), the recognizer could not find a hypothesis with a high enough confidence score. As a result, the recognizer returned a *reject* error to the application. A common response to a rejection is to tell the caller that the system did not understand, and reprompt for the expected information. However, this is not the only approach available to a designer. Often in conversation, when someone does not hear or understand a speaker, a human listener will ask, "What was that?" or "I'm sorry?" We investigated this approach in the context of a speech system, and found that callers actually prefer this *rapid reprompt* strategy to the standard error behavior. It is up to the designer to decide what design strategies are appropriate on an application-by-application basis. Typically, if the caller encounters a second error in either of these situations, the application will describe what it is expecting in more detail. Another important aspect of error recovery is maximum error behavior. If the caller encounters three or four errors in a row, the caller is simply not advancing in the dialog and needs help. In these cases, the application should take the initiative to transfer the struggling caller to an operator or enable the caller to get some other form of assistance.

Designers must be familiar with the technology to understand what its limitations are while making sure the user has a comfortable interaction. One technique that ensures the recognizer understood correctly and boosts the caller's confidence in the system is explicit confirmation. As in the sample dialog above, the system takes information spoken by the user and plays it back for the caller to confirm. If any information is incorrect, the application allows the caller to correct it. In this way, the design of the dialog overcomes the limitations of the technology. All these issues surrounding prompting, universal commands, disambiguation, inference, error handling, and confirmation need to be addressed and specified in the Detailed Design phase of the project.

During Detailed Design, iterative usability is conducted to make sure that the design decisions are intuitive and comfortable for callers. Often, main paths of the application that cover frequently used or important functionality are fleshed out and integrated into a prototype system. One technique to test the design of speech applications is called Wizard of Oz (WOZ). The technique gets its name from the *Wizard of Oz* movie, in which an ordinary man behind a curtain operates the appearance of a powerful wizard. Likewise in the WOZ usability setup, instead of the speech recognition engine and application code leading the caller through a dialog, a human being operates the playing of prompts, creating the appearance of a live speech application. By subtracting the recognition engine and application code from the equation, a prototyped UI can be up and running relatively quickly. As real callers interact with the prompts and dialog flow, they will validate the design decisions as well as make suggestions for improvements. Since no work has been invested in coding up an application at this point, the design changes are easy to make and reduce risk later in the project when changes become much more costly.

Once changes identified by the iterative usability test are integrated into the dialog design specification and all parties have signed off on the final design, the production of the system begins.

2.5 Production

During the Production stage, programmers implement the design and integrate the application with the business' databases. Although C, C++, and Java have all been used to create speech applications, the W3C has been working on a markup language called VoiceXML (http://www.w3.org/TR/voicexml20/), which is becoming the standard for implementing speech applications.

The Production phase also means the development of all aspects of the VUI including the system messages, nonverbal audio, and grammars. The business needs to choose a voice talent to record the system messages. Selecting a voice talent does not necessarily mean choosing the one with the best audition samples. First, the voice has to match the persona defined for the system. The voice also has to sound good over the phone line. Sometimes voices sound great in the studio, but when the audio is downsampled, certain consonants may become distorted for a particular speaker. The voice actor must also be able to control his or her voice. This is extremely important when recording words or phrases that will be concatenated dynamically. Often the prosody, or the way that the words and phrases are delivered, needs to be precise so that prompt sections flow when pieced together. Finally, the actor must be coachable. If the prompt writer has envisioned a certain style of speaking or a certain prosodic contour over a particular phrase, the voice talent needs to be able to accurately fulfill these requests.

Once the voice talent is selected, the voice coach, sound engineer, and voice talent all prepare for prompt recording. A description of the persona and a prompt script should be available to the actor several days before the recording session so that the portrayal of the system persona is accurate and consistent. Since context is so important in conversation, as with speech systems, the prompts need to be listed in a logical order, with sections of concatenated prompt phrases commented with detailed descriptions and cues about how the words and phrases should be delivered. An alphabetical list may be convenient when cataloguing prompts, but this organization is not conducive to smoothly flowing system messages in the final product. The audio files need to be processed so that they are optimal for a speech application. In general, this means downsampling them to 8k.

Nonverbal audio also needs to be in a suitable format to play over a phone line. Often music or natural sounds that work in the sound studio may be difficult to distinguish over the phone, especially if mixed with prompt text.

Grammars are developed in parallel with the production of the prompts and application. The grammar developer uses the dialog specification to understand what utterances the grammar should cover in response to each prompt. All the different ways callers typically express themselves are considered. The developer's job is to ensure that the coverage is thorough and realistic, and to optimize recognition accuracy. The grammars are also checked for overgeneration. The developer removes utterances the caller would never say and also eliminates any ambiguity that the system is not designed to handle. Finally, parameters that need to be modified from the default setting are adjusted. For example, when long digit strings are expected, the endpointing parameters need to be extended since callers sometimes pause between groups of three or four numbers. Once development is complete, the developer prepares the grammars for use in the application and sends them off to the implementers so that the application can be tested.

2.6 Tuning and Validation

Once in the Tuning and Validation phase, the application is complete with prompt recordings, nonverbal audio, and grammars. The code is written and goes through several rounds of bug fixes. As a part of this process, dialog designers call into the system and exhaustively traverse every dialog state and identify any areas where the application behavior does not match the logic defined in the dialog specification. After application testing, a handful of people call into the system for a recognition test. Each person is supplied with a list of what to say. The purpose of the test is to catch any glaring problems with the recognizer (such as inappropriate parameter settings) and make sure the recognition is within an acceptable range. It is important to fix glaring recognition problems at this early phase so that they do not taint other important tests such as evaluative usability and pilot tuning.

When tuning the application, both qualitative and quantitative analyses of the system are important. Evaluative usability testing offers qualitative data, while a pilot with real callers provides objective, quantitative data. These two types of measures contribute to a richer understanding of the application as a whole. Controlled usability taps the subjective impressions of callers as they are using the system. After interacting with the system, callers are asked to state how much they agree or disagree to a series of statements about the system, as in the following example:

I felt that the system understood what I said.

Strongly Disagree	Disagree	Disagree Somewhat	Neither Agree nor Disagree	Agree Somewhat	Agree	Strongly Agree
1	2	3	4	5	6	7
□	□	□	□	□	□	□

Usability specialists can also probe for feedback after each task to understand why callers might have been confused or frustrated. Usability for speech systems is different from those with GUIs because everything is auditory. As such, certain techniques, such as having the user talk aloud as they are performing a task, cannot be used while interacting with a speech system. The drawback of controlled lab studies is that callers are asked to perform specific tasks and are therefore simulating real use. Callers will approach a confirmation strategy differently when thousands of dollars of their own money is at stake.

In contrast, monitoring live phone calls and collecting field data does reflect real usage patterns. The goal of the pilot study is to have real customers interact with the system and provide enough data to tune the grammars, parameters, dictionary, and of course, the dialog flow. Call log analysis presents a clear picture of where people are calling from, what they use the system for, and how they respond when actual transactions are taking place. This type of quantitative data, however, never probes at the users' thoughts as these interactions are taking place, which is why it is a nice complement to usability tests. In the pilot study, the callers' utterances are transcribed. Then tuning specialists compare what callers actually said to what the recognizer thought they said, and calculate an accuracy score for each grammar. A "hotspot" analysis also shows where there are high numbers of error such as No Speech Timeouts or hang-ups. To tune the system, items in the grammar and dictionary are added and/or removed and different parameter settings are modified. Ideally, after the tuning and validation process, the application will be deemed ready for deployment and will be rolled out to the business' customer base.

It is important for the business' marketing department to plan for the rollout of the speech application. Users often benefit from mailer inserts that map out the general structure of the system and provide key commands. Even acknowledging the new technology in the system itself through special welcome prompts in the first few months of deployment will help callers adopt the new system with enthusiasm.

As an example of how the entire design and development process works, we will look at two case studies with which the authors are personally familiar.

2.7   Case Studies

2.7.1   Overview

Each case study illustrates key design problems and solutions. The case studies included are the Bell Canada voice portal, and Avon's self-serve ordering application called "Fast Talk." The Bell Canada portal was designed exclusively for Bell Mobility's cellular subscribers and is a business-to-consumer application. Avon's "Fast Talk" service is designed for its own representatives, many of whom access the service while mobile. For each case study, we will describe the application, business goals, issues encountered in the VUI design, and how they were resolved. A summary of good design principles for speech mobile applications will follow.

2.7.2   Bell Canada

Bell Canada is the largest telecommunications carrier in Canada. They operate a cellular division called Bell Mobility. In late 2001, Bell Mobility launched a voice portal for their mobile subscribers. The voice portal gave subscribers access to the following services:

News: International, business, entertainment, sports, top stories
Weather: National and International by city
E-mail reading: The required password could be changed or turned off through the
    Web site

Bell Canada's objectives in creating the portal were to generate incremental revenue through increased cellular usage, to increase their number of subscribers, and to showcase a convergent project that used Bell wireless connectivity and content as an effective way to provide services to mobile users. They wanted a bilingual application that would serve both their English and French markets and provide value-added services that reduce "churn." Bell Mobility wireless users were consumers, mostly in the 20–40 year old age range, in medium to high household income brackets. They were moderate technology users familiar with email and the Internet. Users wanted convenient and quick access to services that were efficient and easy to use when on the road.

Bell developed a persona, or character, for the voice portal that was inline with their brand image and that reflected key user perceptions about Bell Mobility. The persona needed to be helpful, innovative, and free-spirited, while also empowering users.

An initial design for the portal was usability tested in November 2001, using a "Wizard of Oz" prototype. This type of prototype used a Web interface to play prompts over the phone to a user. As discussed above, the Wizard of Oz technique is a low cost, fairly high fidelity means of obtaining input on design choices and persona before coding begins. The user has the experience of listening to a live application and reacts to the system appropriately. The designer is able to try out and eliminate or refine design choices by seeing how callers respond to the system. In this first test of the portal design by actual Bell Mobility subscribers, two major issues were uncovered.

Navigation was not intuitive throughout application. Users did not know what they could say to get to the main menu, to get from one vertical to the next, to get help, or even to leave the application. They were not used to speaking to a computer and as a result, were not sure what they should say to the system to be understood. Users also hesitated to interrupt the prompts because they did not know if they could barge in and say what they wanted before the prompt ended. The universal navigation commands needed to be clearly communicated to the user either at the beginning of the application or during error recovery. Even if the users could have guessed what the universals would be, in the moment of the interaction, the situation was unfamiliar enough to them that the commands needed to be made explicit.

Secondly, users did not have a clear mental model, or metaphor of how email should work over the phone. During initial use, participants were confused about whether the email reader was really an email feature or a voice mailbox. They did not know where the message would actually be sent to and in what form; they were uncertain whether the original message would be attached when replying or forwarding an email. It became clear that additional confirmation states were needed in the design to let users know exactly what was happening to their messages. Users also had an interesting response to the text-to-speech read-back of messages. Users were sophisticated enough to understand that it was a computer reading back the message, but they expected the voice to be the same gender as the person who sent the message. In other words, several users felt it was "weird" to have a female voice reading back a message from a male sender they knew or vice versa.

Because the design was still at the beginning of the detailed design phase, and the application had not yet been coded, changes could be made easily. The design was changed to make the navigation commands more explicit. Error recovery incorporated more explicit context sensitive help. The email function was streamlined, and confirmation messages were added. The application was retested in January 2002 with a second group of Bell Mobility subscribers. When asked about ease of use, callers gave the application a rating of 6.2 out of 7 (where 7 is the highest positive rating). For general user satisfaction, they rated it 6.7 out of 7. The application is currently in use in Canada.

2.7.3 Avon

Avon is the world's largest beauty company with 500,000 US representatives and two million representatives worldwide. They provide their beauty products directly to their clients through their representatives. The representatives then contact Avon to place and track the orders. Currently Avon has the following channels for inquiry and order entry: a Web site, touch tone system, live agent call center, and most recently, the "Fast Talk" speech recognition application.

In 1999, Avon's existing touch tone IVR (Interactive Voice Response) system experienced a diminishing call volume. In response, Avon decided to implement a speech recognition service that would handle the increased complexity of business functions that a touch tone system does not handle well. Their goal was to "create a compelling alternative to live service." Avon wanted to increase automation on tasks that did not require Customer Service intervention – especially order status, order entry, account information (including balance and account history), product availability, and payments.

However, Avon had a challenge in that their representatives do not fit the high tech adopter profile. On the contrary, they are a challenging user group, especially for speech recognition, for several reasons:

- They are highly distributed geographically with a multiplicity of regional accents and styles of speaking.
- Most are women with little or no technology experience (but many use cell phones).
- The group spans a wide age range (early 20s through 80s) and also a range of educational backgrounds.
- Many do not stay in the position very long (100 percent representative turnover every year) and consequently do not build up their expertise over time.
- In addition, Avon has a complex internal set of "campaigns" that feature different products with potentially different prices and discounts. This adds to the complexity of placing an order.

Avon was fortunate to have a very savvy and experienced project manager who really knew the customer service and automated systems area in Avon. The first iteration of the speech recognition system was developed in English and Spanish during the summer of 2000 and rolled out in October to a limited pilot group of 400–500 representatives around Rye, NY and Springdale, OH. The application was not well accepted in the first pilot.

In January 2001, Avon requested an expert review and redesign of the call flow and dialog for the speech application. Present at that meeting were Avon decision makers and customer service specialists, Syntellect designers and project managers (Syntellect was the system designer and integrator), and a Nuance usability expert (Nuance furnished the speech recognition engine). The meeting was interesting because in the space of a day, consensus was achieved on a new, streamlined call flow that is very close to what is in service today.

What became evident right away was that the main menu structure was based on Avon's internal departmental structure: the way they were organized, versus what the representatives were calling about or wanted to accomplish. Some of the main menu terms were ones used extensively inside the company, but not as much within the representative's group. In other words, the main menu structure did not reflect the representative's mental model.

To get a clearer understanding of what that model could be, several customer service agents (called specialists within Avon) who had a great deal of experience answering representatives on the phone were debriefed by the group. This elicited the set of the most frequently asked questions or requests for assistance with some approximate frequency of how often that request was asked. These were grouped in several "buckets" according to the type of the task and the buckets were renamed with commonly used terms (terms the representatives used when speaking on the phone to specialists). The buckets became the basis for the main menu and submenus structure. Note that this type of exercise is similar to the card sort techniques that are often done during the initial design period. If more time had been available, other techniques such as task analysis and observation could have been used. In general, customer service agents are a very good source of user and task information, and should be consulted in any customer care application early in the design phase. Often users are trained to respond in a certain way because the agent follows a particular protocol in answering the phone. If this protocol is both efficient and elicits good customer satisfaction, it becomes a model that the speech system should consider, or at least be aware of, as it may provide an interface with the least learning curve for the user.

While redesigning the speech application with this new menu structure, two other important elements became clear. The speech system could be simplified considerably, leading to less cognitive load and faster throughput, and the error recovery throughout the application needed to be improved. To help simplify the application, complex but low volume functions were eliminated (based on specialist feedback). Error recovery prompts were made more consistent and additional help functionality, including context sensitive help, was introduced as part of the error recovery to better assist the users.

Finally, given the rapid turnover of the representatives, the group explored some additional representative training methods such as mailers and worksheets.

What happened? The redesign was well accepted by the Avon representatives who tried it, and the application was subsequently rolled out throughout the United States. The system was tuned, and accuracy levels remained high, with about 96.5 percent recognition accuracy and 91.1 percent of the utterance in grammar overall, despite regional speech patterns. The speech system exceeded Avon's target usage and success rate goals immediately. In terms of usage, about 45 percent of the representatives overall choose to use the speech system and about 76 percent of the transactions were completed successfully. Avon monitored calls into the specialists to see if these calls could have been handled by the speech system. They found that the majority of callers were going to specialists for functions not provided in the application.

However, the story goes on: After the national rollout, Avon noticed that there was a slight drop in the number of successfully completed calls, especially in the order entry functionality. To verify what was going on, several approaches were taken:

- Call Monitoring – A usability expert listened to 130 calls and categorized the major user and design issues observed.
- Call Back Interviews – 17 of the representatives who had their calls observed were interviewed to obtain subjective feedback.
- Tuning Analysis – Recognition tuning was undertaken concurrently to understand how the system was performing.

The goal was to understand what was occurring both from the user and the system point of view.

What emerged was unexpected. Analysis showed that most usability issues were not system performance issues involving speech recognition. In fact, system accuracy was 97.1 percent with an in-grammar rate of 92.3 percent. This is quite high for a system with complex order entry functionality. Was it a user acceptance issue? All the representatives interviewed preferred Fast Talk to the previous touch tone system or to waiting on hold for a specialist.

However, more subtle issues were uncovered through call monitoring observation. Fully 30 percent of the observed calls were not completed because the user was not ready to input the order numbers and was missing information the system needed to complete the task. Also, in the feedback gathered, users mentioned that the system was missing important functionality and this made them more inclined to speak to a specialist instead of using the speech system. Many also said that they were never shown how to use the system. They mentioned that even a quick run-through would have been beneficial.

In response to this study, Avon increased the system's capacity to pause and allowed more time for callers to respond to the prompts. They added functionality for both order status and product availability, and most importantly, undertook a massive education campaign to support Fast Talk, including an instructional CD and planner inserts with tips on how to use the system for representatives. A follow up survey among the representatives elicited positive response:

- 26 percent said that they were satisfied with the system as is.
- 51 percent felt they would use Fast Talk for over 50 percent of their service needs.
- 84 percent said that the planner insert was extremely useful.

Avon continues to refine the system with continual in-service call monitoring. They document all user and system problems that arise. Now, in addition to monitoring calls into the specialists, supervisors are required to monitor calls coming into the speech application 50 percent of the time. Continual monitoring enables Avon to stay in touch with evolving business needs and caller requirements, and identify areas where enhancements would be beneficial. Ongoing statistics are maintained to identify usage trends. Periodic gatherings of Avon representative are used as well to obtain additional feedback.

What was the payback? In identifying user issues continually throughout the development process, applying solutions and continuing to monitor user reactions, Avon exceeded projected revenue by 50 percent the first year after deployment. They had anticipated planned savings of $1.2 million, but they achieved an actual savings of $1.9 million. The speech system was instrumental in increasing automation in a way that the representatives accepted. In 2001, 2.8 million calls were completed. That number increased to 3.6 million calls in 2002, with even more forecasted for 2003.

From both these case studies, many lessons were learned with regard to both the process and the design of the voice user interface.

2.8   Guidelines

2.8.1   What Are the General Process Guidelines We Can Extract from These Two Case Studies?

One of the most important is to *use the tried and tested project method*. By gathering thorough requirements, iterating design, and validating user experience, major changes can be addressed early in the process.

It is especially important to *gather user requirements prior to design*. Include information on how users are interacting with existing communication channels and how each differs in terms of user segments. Speak to customer service representatives or others that receive customer calls to find out the type and frequency of calls received. Find out how and in what sequence users are doing the tasks you want to automate as input to your design and what terms or terminology they use. Ask the marketing/market research departments to provide you with their user segments for the company and each segment's characteristics and known needs.

Another very important guideline is to *focus on the right functionality* for your application when gathering system requirements. Because voice is ephemeral and there are no visual references, concentrate only on the key 80/20 tasks that are meaningful to automate for both company and user, and iterate the design until the application is easy to use and task completion is high. Save details for the Web site.

Obtain feedback from users throughout the design phase and *continue monitoring users* after deployment. As we saw from the Avon case study, collecting ongoing reactions from real callers helps to optimize the design and increase user acceptance, task completion, and customer satisfaction.

Prepare for the deployment of the system. Let users know ahead of time that they will be talking to a speech system. Provide a visual overview of the system for first time use if the application is complex. This can be a wallet card or other visual aid that helps the user form a mental map of the system. This is especially useful for non-native speakers as they can see what terms are used and therefore know what to say to the system at each step in the call flow to be well recognized.

2.8.2   What Design Guidelines Are Particular to the Mobile User?

Design with a clear metaphor in mind and make that metaphor known to the user, especially if the functionality is complex, like email or unified messaging. As we saw in the Bell Canada example, taking something visual like email, and bringing it into the auditory modality can be tricky. When introducing new functionality, let callers know what is happening every step of the way and be clear on how they need to respond.

Make sure that the users' mental model is reflected in the system's menu structure and call flow. The users' cognitive load needs to be low, especially in a mobile situation where they are often multitasking (driving a car, walking, and so on). To this end, make sure menu terms and choices are immediately clear and meaningful to the user (which may or may not follow the way the business is organized). Also, design the flow of questions so that they are relevant and close to what callers are used to. Don't ask mobile users to learn new habits on the fly.

Be explicit about the navigation and universal commands. Do not make users guess.

Let callers pause the system if necessary. As we saw in the Avon case study, mobile users need more time to collect information when on the go.

Provide sufficient error recovery and context sensitive help so that the user is not left high and dry and feeling frustrated. This is even more important in a mobile situation where high noise levels in the environment can make recognition more difficult. Error recovery prompts should be written in a natural conversational style to help comprehension.

The lessons learned from the case studies demonstrate the power of a good voice user interface. Many deficiencies in deployed systems these days are caused not so much by the technology as by the dialog design. Even though much research on good design practices is still needed, we make strides toward a better understanding of the human-computer interaction with speech technology with each deployment.

2.9 References

Dutton, R.T., Foster, J.C., and Jack, M.A. (1999). Please mind the doors: Do interface metaphors improve the usability of voice response services? BT Technological Journal, 17(1), 172–177.

LeDuc, N., Dougherty, M., and Ankaitis, V. (2001). Measuring the performance of speech applications: A user-centered approach. Proceedings of UAHCI 2001, Universal Access in Human-Computer Interaction, 372–376.

Reeves, B. and Nass, C. (1996). The media equation: How people treat computers, television, and new media like real people and places. New York: CSLI Publications.

Chapter 3

Designing J2ME™ Applications: MIDP and UI Design

Annette Wagner, Cynthia Bloch

3.1 Introduction

The Java™ 2 Platform, Micro Edition (J2ME™) is the Java platform for consumer and embedded devices such as mobile phones, PDAs, television set-top boxes, and other embedded devices. Like its counterparts – Java™ 2 Platform, Enterprise Edition (J2EE™ platform), Java™ 2 Platform, Standard Edition (J2SE™ platform), and Java Card™ – the J2ME platform is a set of standard Java APIs defined through the Java Community Process™ program. The Java Community Process program uses expert groups that include leading device manufacturers, software vendors, and service providers to create the standard APIs.

This chapter provides an overview of the J2ME platform architecture, and of MIDP. It then describes a process for creating a MIDP application. It covers the use of the MIDP user interface components and some issues in deploying your application.

3.2 J2ME Platform Architecture

The J2ME platform includes a flexible user interface, a robust security model, a broad range of built-in network protocols, and support for both networked and disconnected applications. With the J2ME platform, applications are written once for a wide range of devices, are downloaded dynamically, and leverage each device's native capabilities.

The J2ME platform architecture defines *configurations*, *profiles*, and *optional packages* as elements for building complete Java runtime environments that meet the requirements for a broad range of devices and target markets. Figure 3.1 shows the relationships between these elements. Each combination is optimized for the memory, processing power, and I/O capabilities of a related category of devices. The result is a common Java platform that fully leverages each type of device to deliver a rich user experience. The following sections define the terms configurations,

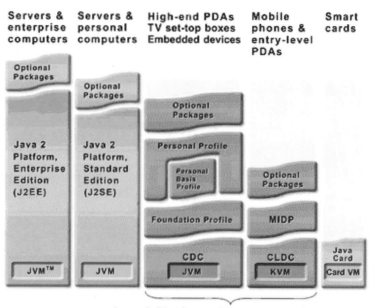

Servers &   Servers &   High-end PDAs   Mobile   Smart
enterprise   personal   TV set-top boxes   phones &   cards
computers   computers   Embedded devices   entry-level
                                                     PDAs

Java 2 Platform, Micro Edition (J2ME)

Figure 3.1   J2ME platform architecture

profiles, and optional packages, and discuss them in terms of the Mobile Information Device Profile (MIDP).

3.2.1   Configurations

Configurations are composed of a virtual machine and a minimal set of class libraries. They provide the base functionality for a particular range of devices that share similar characteristics, such as network connectivity and memory footprint. Currently, there are two J2ME configurations: the Connected Limited Device Configuration (CLDC), and the Connected Device Configuration (CDC).

CLDC is the smaller of the two configurations; it is the configuration on which MIDP is built. CLDC was designed for devices with intermittent network connections, slow processors, and limited memory – devices such as mobile phones, two-way pagers, and PDAs. These devices typically have both 16- or 32-bit CPUs and a minimum of 128 KB to 512 KB of memory available for the Java platform implementation and associated applications.

3.2.2   Profiles

In order to provide a complete runtime environment targeted at specific device categories, configurations must be combined with a set of higher level APIs, or profiles, that further define the application life cycle model, the user interface, and access to device specific properties.

The Mobile Information Device Profile (MIDP) is designed for small devices such as mobile phones and entry-level PDAs. It offers the core functionality required by mobile applications, including the user interface, network connectivity, local data storage, and application management. Combined with CLDC, MIDP provides a complete Java runtime environment that leverages the capabilities of handheld devices and minimizes both memory and power consumption.

3.2.3 Optional Packages

Device manufacturers can extend the J2ME platform by adding optional packages to configurations and their profiles. Optional packages are standard APIs created to address very specific market requirements for using existing and emerging technologies such as Bluetooth, Web services, wireless messaging, multimedia, and database connectivity. Because optional packages are modular, device manufacturers can include them as needed to fully leverage the features of each device.

3.3 MIDP Overview

MIDP, with CLDC, provides the Java runtime environment for mobile information devices such as phones and entry-level PDAs. It is deployed globally on millions of mobile phones and PDAs, and supported by leading Java technology integrated development environments (IDEs).

MIDP enables developers to create applications that provide great end user experiences on mobile information devices. MIDP applications can operate in both networked and disconnected modes, and have the ability to securely store and manage data locally. In addition, MIDP applications are graphical. The MIDP graphical user interface is optimized for the small display sizes, input methods, and other native features of mobile devices. MIDP provides intuitive navigation and data entry by leveraging the phone keypads, small QWERTY keyboards, and extra buttons such as arrow keys and touch screens.

3.3.1 MIDP Features

MIDP includes features such as user interface capabilities, multimedia and game functionality, network connectivity, over-the-air provisioning (OTA), and security, as shown in Figure 3.2.

User Interface
MIDP features a high-level user interface API that shields developers from the complexity of building applications for mobile devices that have different capabilities, such as user input methods and display sizes. The high-level API enables developers to build easy to use, highly graphical applications that can be run on multiple mobile devices without code changes. The portability of MIDP applications reduces development effort and speeds deployment.

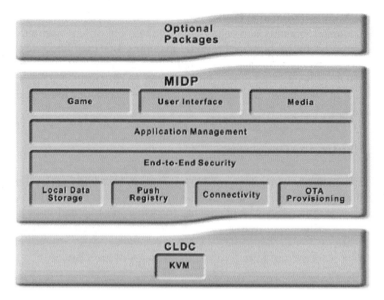

Figure 3.2   MIDP features

MIDP high-level user interface functionality includes predefined screens for displaying and selecting lists, editing text, popping up alert dialogs, adding scrolling tickers, as well as displaying and editing forms. Forms are screens that can include any number of predefined items. The items can include images, read-only text fields, editable text fields, editable date and time fields, gauges, and choice groups. Developers can also define custom items to provide unique functionality and graphics. (It is up to the developer to make sure that a custom item is portable.)

All high-level screens and items are device aware, with built-in support for the native display size, input, and navigation capabilities. This enables developers to define a highly portable, flexible user interface that automatically changes its layout and navigation to fully leverage each device.

The MIDP user interface also has a low-level API for developers who need more control over the screen. Using this API makes it more difficult to write portable applications, but it can be done with care.

Whether a developer uses the high- or low-level APIs, the components will not have overlapping windows. The MIDP user interface APIs were designed for devices with small screens and limited or absent windowing capability. It is not a desktop user interface toolkit.

Multimedia and Game Functionality

A low-level user interface API for building portable games and multimedia applications API complements the high-level API. The low-level user interface API gives developers greater control of graphics and input, but requires that they take care to make their user interface portable. A game API adds game-specific functionality (such as sprites and tiled layers) that takes advantage of native device graphics capabilities. A built-in audio building block provides support for tones, tone sequences, and WAV files. In addition, developers can use the Mobile Media API (MMAPI), an optional package for MIDP, to add video and other rich multimedia content. MMAPI was defined in JSR 135.

Connectivity

MIDP enables developers to use the native data network and messaging capabilities of mobile information devices. It supports leading connectivity standards including HTTP, HTTPS, datagram, sockets, server sockets, and serial port communication. MIDP can also support the Wireless Messaging API (JSR-000120), which provides Short Message Service (SMS) and Cell Broadcast Service (CBS) capabilities of GSM and CDMA networks. The Wireless Messaging API (WMA) is an optional package.

MIDP also supports a server push model. A push registry keeps track of applications registered to receive inbound information from the network. When information arrives, the device starts the application based on user preferences. (Users can set preferences that enable the application to be started at any time without asking permission, that enable the application to be started only if they give permission, or that shut off push capability for the application.) This push architecture enables developers to create MIDP applications that include alerts, messaging, and broadcasts, and that leverage the event-driven capabilities of devices and carrier networks.

Over-the-Air Provisioning

A major benefit of MIDP is its ability to dynamically deploy and update applications over-the-air. MIDP also enables a service provider to identify which MIDP applications will work on a given device, and obtain status reports from the device following installation, updates, or removal.

To download a MIDP application, users browse lists of applications stored on Web servers. Once a user selects an application, the device does some basic checks; for example, the device checks to see whether it has enough space to store the application. If the application passes the initial tests, the device downloads, verifies, and installs the application. Users can easily update and remove any installed application.

End-to-End Security

MIDP provides a robust security model that protects the network, applications, and mobile information devices. The model is built on open standards; it uses HTTPS, which leverages existing standards such as SSL and WTLS to enable the transmission of encrypted data. Security domains protect against unauthorized access of data, applications, and other network and device resources by MIDP applications on the device. By default, MIDP applications are not trusted, and are assigned to untrusted domains that prevent access to any privileged functionality. To gain privileged access, a MIDP application must be assigned to specific domains that are defined on the mobile device, and are properly signed using the X.509 PKI security standard.

In order for a signed MIDP application to be downloaded, installed, and granted associated permissions, it must be successfully authenticated.

3.3.2 MIDP Device Requirements

Devices that run MIDP need these minimum hardware characteristics:

Display
- Screen size of 96 × 54 pixels
- Display depth of 1-bit
- Pixel shape (aspect ratio) of approximately 1 : 1
- Input through one or more of the following methods:
    - One-handed keyboard (ITU-T phone keypad)
    - Two-handed keyboard, (QWERTY keyboard)
    - Touch screen

Memory
- 256 kilobytes of nonvolatile memory for the MIDP components
- 8 kilobytes of nonvolatile memory for application-created persistent data
- 128 kilobytes of volatile memory for the Java runtime environment

Networking capabilities
- Two-way
- Wireless
- Possibly intermittent
- Limited bandwidth

Sound
- Ability to play tones, either with dedicated hardware or a software algorithm

3.4   MIDP Application Overview

Applications created for the MIDP environment are consumer applications. The applications can be for business functions (such as a troubleshooting application to help assembly line supervisors debug problems), information access and communication (such as an address book from which you might dial a phone number), and entertainment (such as a game to play while you are standing in line at a store).

3.4.1 Consumer Characteristics

Consumers have different characteristics than users of desktop systems. Consumers are familiar with appliances that typically have simple, predictable user interfaces (such as phones, microwave ovens, and remote controls), and might feel uncomfortable dealing with anything they consider to be too "high-tech." They expect consumer products to be predictable, easy to learn, and easy to use.

Consumers should be able to predict what will happen when they take an action; they rarely look at documentation. For example, assume that an address book application and an e-mail application on a mobile phone have menus that display the available operations, and the address book has a list element called New Entry for adding a record. The question for the e-mail application is whether its list element for writing a new message should be called Write or New Message. Using New Message is parallel to New Entry in the address book, which makes it an attractive option. It makes the address book and e-mail applications more consistent. Consumers, though, do not think about creating a new message; they think of writing to someone. For them, Write might be a better predictor of the command's behavior.

If you must choose between predictable and efficient, choose predictable. Predictability is a better investment than efficiency. Usability testing has shown that consumers are much happier with systems that are predictable, even when they are not as efficient.

3.4.2 Characteristics of Consumer Products

A consumer device typically has less memory, smaller or lower resolution displays, fewer colors, and different I/O mechanisms than personal computers. It is important to consider the limited resources and particular input and output (I/O) mechanisms of the device when designing applications for them.

Application designers and developers should be aware of:

* Device specifications
* Deployment concerns (See "Handling Deployment and Usage Issues")
* Any network operator requirements and network latency concerns

3.5 Creating a MIDP Application

When developing an application for MIDP, application designers use screens to organize their user interfaces into manageable tasks. That is, a MIDP application is a set of screens, each enabling the consumer to carry out one or more tasks. Some tasks could lead to other screens, some could update data on the user's device, and so on. Consumers interact on a screen-by-screen basis with their applications.

An early task for application designers, then, after creating a usage case for their application, is identifying the tasks that the users will accomplish with it. For example, SmartTicket, an application that enables users to buy movie tickets from their mobile devices, could be made up, in part, of these tasks:

* Choosing a movie
* Finding a theater
* Rating movies
* Buying tickets
* Viewing movie show times

To map the tasks to screens, application designers typically create storyboards. The storyboards do not contain low-level details, such as how users will operate the device to do the tasks. Instead, they concentrate on the screen's purpose and the tasks that it enables the user to perform. For example, the sketches in Figure 3.3 show a partial storyboard for SmartTicket.

Figure 3.3   Partial storyboard for the SmartTicket application

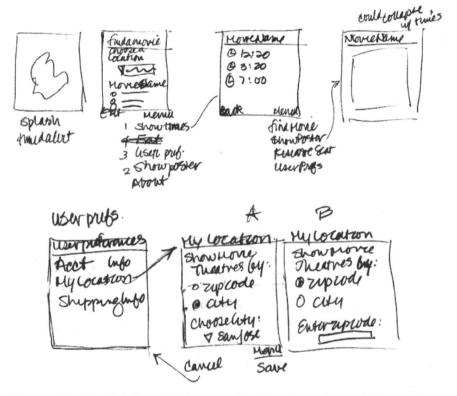

Figure 3.4   Partial SmartTicket application flow derived from story-board

Because application flow is much more critical for MIDP applications than desktop applications, the next thing you should do is to derive application flow. Figure 3.4 shows the application flow derived from some of the SmartTicket sketches.

From the application flow, application designers can create a mock-up of the application screens that map to MIDP user interface components. Each

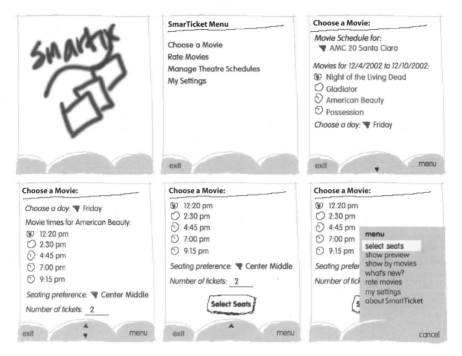

Figure 3.5   Partial mock-up of SmartTicket

screen should handle one or more tasks. Figure 3.5 shows a partial mock-up of SmartTicket.

The mock-up of the application should include navigational devices that MIDP implementers might use, so it will have more screens than the storyboard. It should include screens for any busy indicators in the application, and system menus (lists or menus generated by the MIDP implementation). For example, MIDP implementers often map *abstract commands* to system menus, so the mock-up could contain screens that show a system menu. (Abstract commands are actions that have an interface determined by the MIDP implementation instead of being associated with a specific UI component, such as a list. They are described in more detail in "Using Abstract Commands.")

3.6 Using Abstract Commands

Abstract commands enable application designers to define actions for an application without specifying the accompanying user interface. Instead, MIDP implementers decide how to present abstract commands. Making MIDP implementers responsible for this part of the user interface enables applications to integrate better into the native UIs of a variety of devices, and feel more natural to users. When a MIDP

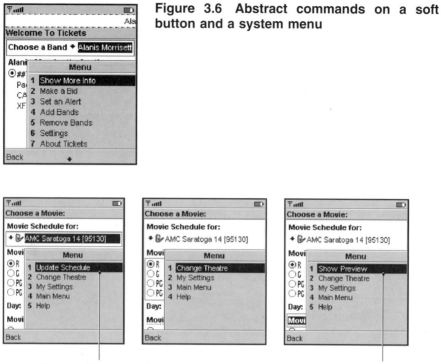

Figure 3.6 Abstract commands on a soft button and a system menu

Figure 3.7 Item-specific abstract commands

application looks and acts like a device-native application, it is easier to learn and use. Giving MIDP implementers the responsibility of creating and laying out MIDP user interface components for their devices enables applications to be both predictable and portable.

You can attach abstract commands to screens and items. Abstract commands associated with the screen are always available to the user. They often appear on soft buttons, on a system menu, or both, as shown in Figure 3.6.

An abstract command associated with an item on a form screen appears only when the item has *focus* (that is, when user's position is at that item). See "High-Level User Interface Components" for more information on forms and their items. Figure 3.7 shows item-specific abstract commands appearing when an item has focus, and changing as the user traverses through the items on the screen.

Sometimes application designers who are used to designing desktop applications (in which the application designer must lay out menu items, buttons, and so on) try to design MIDP application screens that use buttons instead of associating abstract commands with screens. Do *not* give in to this temptation. There are a number of problems with designing MIDP applications that use buttons to the exclusion of associating abstract commands with a screen. One problem is that buttons

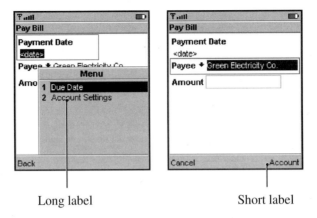

Figure 3.8   Short and long command label

are easily lost when scrolling; users can find it difficult to traverse or scroll to the button in order to select it. Another problem is that buttons do not integrate into the native user interface and the application is therefore less portable and less predictable.

3.6.1   Parts of an Abstract Command

Commands have a type, label, and priority. Labels are shown to users. An abstract command must have a short label, and should also have a long label. The MIDP implementation decides which one to display, typically by checking available space. Figure 3.8 shows the short and long label for a command.

An abstract command's type lets the MIDP implementation know the purpose of the abstract command, so that it can be better mapped onto the device. For example, one type is BACK. If the device has a Back key, the MIDP implementation can assign a command of type BACK to that key. The types of abstract commands are:

- Screen – Commands that affect the entire screen or application. For example, setting application preferences is best thought of as an abstract command of type SCREEN. A screen might have multiple commands of type SCREEN.
- Item – Commands that affect a selected item or element on a screen. For example, if a screen contains a list of movies, the actions to buy a ticket to the selected movie, or to see the selected movie's poster are best thought of as ITEM commands. A screen might have multiple commands of type ITEM.
- OK – Command that gives positive answers to queries. For example, if a query said, "Really delete the file?" the response indicating that the file should be deleted would best be thought of as an abstract command of type OK. The command could have a label of Delete. A screen does not typically have multiple abstract commands of type OK.

- Cancel – Command that gives negative answers to queries. For example, if a query said, "Really delete the file?" the response indicating that the file should not be deleted would best be thought of as an abstract command of type CANCEL. The command could have the label Don't Delete. A screen does not typically have multiple abstract commands of type CANCEL.
- Back – Commands that return users to a previous state in the application. Commands of type BACK could return users to the previous screen, to the start of an action that involves multiple screens, or to the start of the entire application. (The example commands could have the labels Back, Start Over, and Home.) A screen might have multiple commands of type BACK.
- Help – Commands to present useful information about the application to the user. A screen might have multiple abstract commands of type HELP.
- Stop – Command to halt a currently running process within the application. For example, if an application accesses a Web page, stopping the download of the page (for example, because it is taking too long), it would best be thought of as an abstract command of type STOP. A screen does not typically have multiple abstract commands of type STOP.
- Exit – Command for leaving the application. An application should always provide a command of type EXIT command on appropriate screens.

An abstract command's priority lets the MIDP implementation know how important an abstract command is, compared to others of the same type. Using the same example, the MIDP implementation would assign the highest priority command of type BACK to the device's Back key.

When designing the abstract commands associated with a screen (and the items on that screen), order them first by type and then by priority within a type. A screen can have multiple commands of the same type. For example, a screen could have two commands of type HELP: one with a label of About that would show an about box, and another with a label of Help that would provide a help screen. You would probably give the command that provided a help screen a higher priority than the command that provided the about box.

Ordering by type, then priority helps the MIDP implementation present the abstract commands appropriately. Figure 3.9 shows a screen that has three commands of the same type (SCREEN), each with a different priority.

3.6.2 Paired Commands

Abstract commands that appear on the same screen, and have the same type, should have different priorities. The exception, however, is paired commands. Paired commands complement each other. Although they are associated with the same screen or item, they never appear at the same time. Instead, when a user chooses the visible command, the pair other command seems to take its place. Figure 3.10 shows paired commands from SmartTicket.

In order for a MIDP implementation to put both commands of the pair in the same location (so that one can seem to take the place of the other), the commands must have the same type and the same priority.

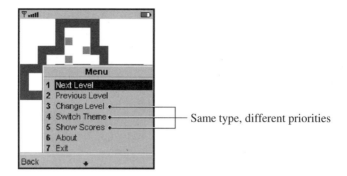

Figure 3.9   Commands of the same type with different priorities

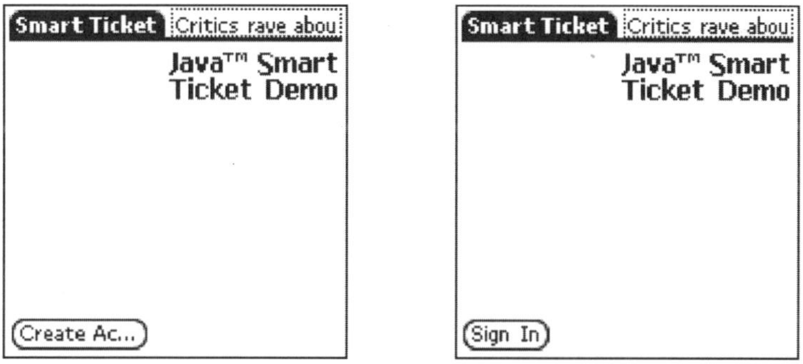

Figure 3.10   Paired commands

3.7   Using MIDP User Interface Components

MIDP applications can use high- and low-level user interface components, as well as abstract commands. This section provides an overview of the user interface components.

3.7.1   High-Level User Interface Components

High-level user interface components are screens dedicated to a specific task, such as entering text, choosing an item from a list, or filling out a form. The components are designed to make applications portable across devices. To achieve portability, MIDP implementers define the visual appearance of the components, such as their shapes. An application that uses these components automatically looks like a native application on any MIDP device.

In addition to visual appearance, the MIDP implementation handles navigation, scrolling, and other primitive interactions. Applications can run on many different devices because they are not aware of these low-level, device-dependent tasks.

The high-level user interface components are forms, lists, text boxes, and alerts. In addition, forms have associated form items.

Forms

Forms are screens that contain one or more form items, as shown in Figure 3.11. (Form items are described in the next section.) A form is typically the main screen used for application design. It is a screen that can contain one or more items, such as gauges, images, and boxes into which the user can enter text.

Use a form to enable users to carry out one large task or one to three small tasks. It should not be more than three to four screens in length. Check the length of your forms on different devices, and test your forms with users to ensure that you are not trying to do too many tasks on a single screen.

Context-Sensitive Forms

Although changes that seem arbitrary to users can lead to problems, context-sensitive forms are understandable and can make forms more usable. Because an application is notified each time a user changes an item, you could create content-sensitive forms that change as a result of user actions. For example, a form could have a check box that determines whether particular items appear. Figure 3.12 shows a form in which more information appears when the user chooses an item from a list (in this case, when the user chooses a theater).

Affecting-Form Layout

Application designers can affect the layout of a form by providing *layout directives* with form items. Layout directives are constants that inform the MIDP implementation of any special instructions for placing the form item on the screen, in relation to the other items.

The LAYOUT_DEFAULT directive enables the MIDP implementation to use the strategy that might provide the best layout for the device. Use this directive whenever possible.

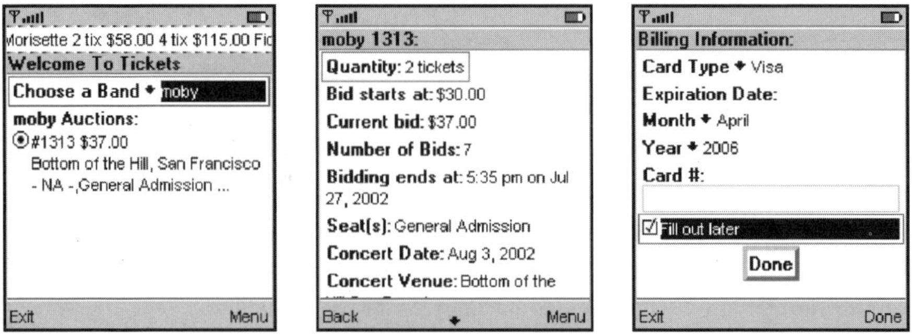

Figure 3.11   Forms

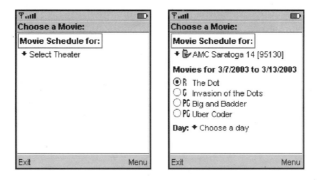

Figure 3.12   Context-sensitive form

The LAYOUT_2 directive instructs the MIDP implementation to use MIDP 2.0 layout rules. Using MIDP 2.0 layout rules, more than one form item can share a row, and string and image items are not required to start a new row. It also enables the MIDP implementation to follow any directives for shrinking and expanding the item, for vertical alignment, and so on.

In addition to the directives that are new for MIDP 2.0, you can use MIDP 1.0 image directives for all form items. For example, the LAYOUT_ NEWLINE_BEFORE and LAYOUT_NEWLINE_AFTER directives can now be used with any item.

Note that the LAYOUT_NEWLINE_BEFORE and LAYOUT_ NEWLINE_AFTER directives result in only a single new line. If an item uses the LAYOUT_NEWLINE_AFTER directive, and the following item uses the LAYOUT_NEWLINE_BEFORE directive, there will not be an empty row. The item with the LAYOUT_NEWLINE_BEFORE directive will simply start a new row. If you want an empty row, for whatever reason, use new-line characters (\n) in string items. You will get one row for each new-line character. (That is, one new-line character would result in the staring a new row, two new-line characters in a row would result in an empty row, and so on.)

Form Items

MIDP provides a variety of form items, including a custom item that you can create if none of the available items meets the needs of your application. The types of form items are choice groups, text fields, date and time fields, gauges, strings, images, and the previously mentioned custom item.

All form items can have a label, preferred size, command, and one or more layout directives. A label is a string associated with a form item. Most of the items on the forms in Figure 3.11 have labels. They are the part of the item shown in bold. (The Done button and the Fill out later check box do not have labels.) An item's preferred size lets the MIDP implementation know the height, width, or both required to optimally display the item. Preferred sizes are typically useful for image items and custom items. Don't provide a preferred size for items that contain text, since you cannot know what font the device will be using. See "Using Abstract Commands" and "Affecting Form Layout" for more information on commands and layout directives.

Choice Groups

There are three kinds of choice groups: *single choice*, *multiple-choice*, and *popup* choice. Figure 3.13 shows all three types of choice groups. Single choice and multiple-choice choice groups correspond to single choice and multiple-choice lists. Implicit lists do not have a corresponding choice group. Use a choice group to enable users to choose among options.

Text Fields

Text fields are similar to text boxes, but appear on a form. They have the same constraints and modifiers described in "Text Boxes." Use a text field to enable users to enter text. Figure 3.14 shows text fields on a form.

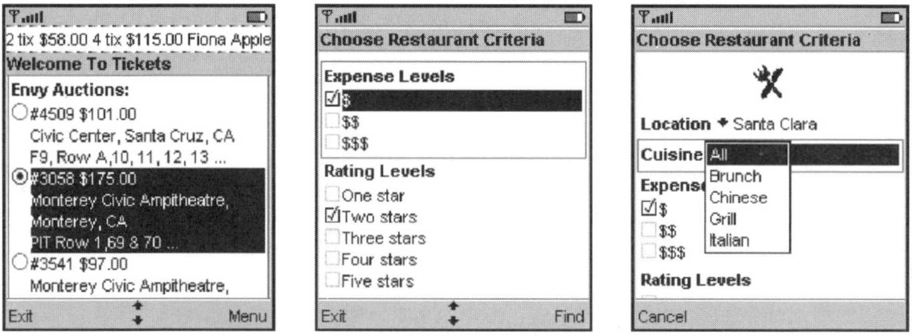

Figure 3.13   Choice groups on a form

Figure 3.14   Text fields on a form

Date-Time Field

A date-time field can be set to show the date, time, or both. The user can always edit the displayed value. Sometimes the date and time are edited off the form screen on a separate screen, as shown in Figure 3.15.

Gauges

Gauges can be interactive or noninteractive. Interactive gauges enable users to set values like volume control. Figure 3.16 shows an interactive gauge. Use a small range of values for an interactive gauge, so it can be mapped more easily to a small display.

Noninteractive gauges provide feedback to the user. There are three kinds of noninteractive gauges: *progress*, *incremental*, and *continuous*. Figure 3.17 shows a progress and an incremental gauge. Each are suited for different contexts, depending upon how much information is available.

String and Image Items

String and image items provide static information to the user (that is, the user cannot edit a string or an image). Strings and images are available in three modes: *plain*, *button*, and *hyperlink*, as shown in Figure 3.18. The plain appearance mode simply displays the string or image. Button mode turns strings and images into interactive

Figure 3.15   A date-time field on a form

Figure 3.16   An interactive gauge on a form

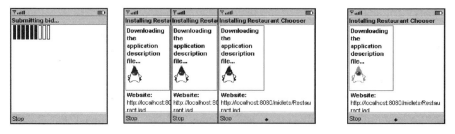

Figure 3.17   A progress gauge and an incremental gauge on a form

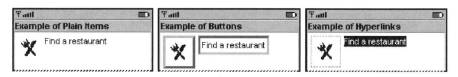

Figure 3.18   The three modes of string and image items on forms

Figure 3.19   A custom item

buttons. Use buttons cautiously on forms that require scrolling. Associate a command with the button so that selecting the button performs a task. Hyperlink mode turns strings and images into hyperlinks. Hyperlinks are not links to the Web, but rather links to screens in the MIDP application so that users can access related information. Like buttons, you must associate a command with the hyperlink so that selecting the hyperlink brings the user to a new screen.

Custom Items

A custom item is provided to enable you to create your own component. It is similar to having a small canvas on a form screen. Figure 3.19 shows custom items. If you create a custom item, integrate it with the native user interface, with respect to traversal, colors, fonts, and layout.

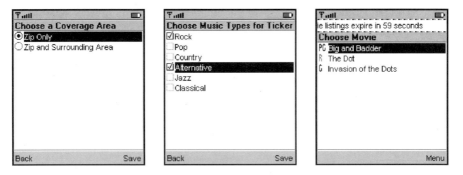

Figure 3.20   List types

Lists

There are three list types: *single-choice*, which allows the user to select one and only one element; *multiple-choice*, which allows the user to select zero or more elements; and *implicit*, which allows the user to select one element and take an action on it.

Use an single choice list when one choice must be selected. An single choice list begins with one item selected and, if the user selects an item, that item becomes selected and the previous selection is cleared. Use a multiple-choice list when the user can choose zero or more zero elements. If the user selects an element, the element changes its state from selected to cleared, or vice versa. (You can use a multiple-choice list with a single element to enable the user to toggle the state of a property, such as whether to use sound.) Use an implicit list for menu-style screens.

Text Boxes

Use a text box when you need a full screen for text editing or display. A text box can have constraints and modifiers. Constraints are restrictive values. For example, one constraint, NUMERIC, limits input to numbers. Other constraints are ANY, DECIMAL, PHONENUMBER, EMAIL, and URL. (There is no way for a device to validate an e-mail address or URL. You must have your application check the actual value contents of the text field if you require a properly formed value.)

Modifiers can be combined with each other or with a constraint to further affect the text box or field's behavior. For example, one modifier, PASSWORD, masks the user's input. Other modifiers are UNEDITABLE, INITIAL_CAPS_SENTENCE, INITIAL_CAPS_WORD, NON_PREDICTIVE, and SENSITIVE.

Alerts

An alert is a screen that communicates information to users, such as errors or status messages. An alert can be *timed* or *modal*. The device dismisses a timed alert after a period of time, while a user must dismiss a modal alert. An alert can contain an image, a gauge, a string, and abstract commands. Especially on a small display, an

Figure 3.21   A text box   **Figure 3.22   A confirmation alert**

alert might need to scroll. If an alert needs to scroll, it will be a modal alert, even if you requested that the alert be timed.

There are five kinds of alerts: *info*, *warning*, *error*, *confirmation*, and *alarm*. Their names describe their purposes. A MIDP implementation can distinguish the different types of alerts with different sounds, different looks, or whatever is appropriate for the device. Use alert types so that your application takes advantage of the presentation styles for the different types of alerts on the device. Giving the user visual and auditory cues as to the nature of an alert can make applications easier to use.

3.7.2   Low-Level User Interface Components

Low-level screen components give you more control over the screen. It is more difficult to write portable applications with these components but, with care, you can do it. MIPD has two low-level user interface components: canvas and game canvas. A canvas is the more general screen. Game canvas is designed for use in games.

Canvases

A canvas is useful for situations where a custom item on a form screen won't work. For example, if you need maximum display area, you could use a canvas in full-screen mode. Full-screen mode removes any title, ticker, and perhaps other items a MIDP implementation might display to the user, such as a battery power indicator. As another example, you could use a canvas to enable the user to edit a custom item off the form.

Game Canvases

A game canvas adds sprites, tiling, layers, and a backing store to a regular canvas. Use it for games and at any other time that you feel its additional features would be helpful.

Figure 3.23   A canvas

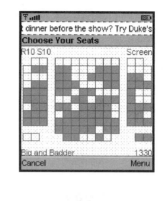

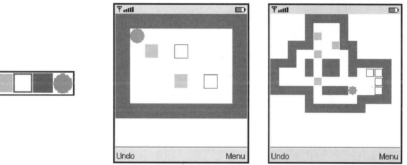

Figure 3.24   A set of tiles, and two game canvases that use them

3.8   Handling Deployment and Usage Issues

A device must have a way for users to find and install new applications, run them, remove them, and so on. These tasks are called application management, and are the responsibility of MIDP implementers. (See "Over The Air User Initiated Provisioning Specification for the Mobile Information Device Profile," which is part of the *MIDP 2.0 Specification*.)

Although application designers cannot affect a device's application management, they can help users by taking care in naming their applications, providing an icon that a device's application management system can use to represent the application for the user, and so on.

3.8.1   Presentation Issues

Many devices use icons to represent applications to the user, and should also provide default icons for applications that do not have icons of their own. To uniquely represent your application, provide 12 × 12 pixel, color icons in PNG format that devices can show to users. The icons should also look good displayed in grayscale.

You can provide one icon for the MIDP application suite and one icon for each MIDP application.

Devices also provide the name of your application to the user. They do this when displaying screens that enable the user to manage (install, update, delete, and so on) applications, and when displaying a list of applications that the user can launch. Name your MIDP application suite and MIDP applications so that users can tell what they contain. It can be hard for users to remember what is in an application with a generic name like Demos and Examples. In addition, remember that there may not be space to display the full name of your application. Name it so that the user can tell what it is, even if only the first part of the name can be displayed.

3.8.2 Size Issues

Try to minimize the sizes of the files that users will have to install on their devices. Small devices have limited resources. Applications that use less storage space conserve device resources and can start faster. In addition, they could also save the user money: smaller applications take less time to download.

One way to minimize the size of your application is to minimize the size of your graphics files. Save the images with only the colors they need. The fewer colors an image contains, the smaller its file size. Provide a color image that looks good in grayscale instead of providing both a color and a grayscale version of the same image.

3.9 Conclusion

Creating a great user experience on a small consumer device can be a difficult task for even the most experienced designers. Challenges include everything from display size to consumer mindset. If you have only one goal in mind, that goal should be one of simplicity. True simplicity takes iteration and commitment to achieve, but pays off in the end. Consumers will love your product if it is truly simple to use.

This chapter has given you a starting point for understanding how to design MIDP applications. See the *MIDP 2.0 Style Guide* for a more in-depth explanation of how to work with the MIDP technology. In addition, to use the Web to learn more about the J2ME platform and MIDP, see:

http://java.sun.com/products/midp (MIDP Portal)
http://java.sun.com/j2me/docs/alt-html/midp-style-guide7/index.html   (MIDP   1.0
    Style Guide)
http://jcp.org (Java Community Process)
http://jcp.org/en/jsr/detail?id=37 (MIDP 1.0 Specification)
http://jcp.org/en/jsr/detail?id=118 (MIDP 2.0 Specification)
http://jcp.org/en/jsr/detail?id=135 (MMAPI Specification)
http://jcp.org/en/jsr/detail?id=120 (WMA Specification)

http://java.sun.com/j2me (J2ME Portal)
http://developers.sun.com/techtopics/mobility (Wireless Developer Portal)
http://java.sun.com/j2me/docs (Technical white papers and other information on the
    J2ME platform)

Chapter 4

Designing Multimodal Applications

David Cuka, Tasos Anastasakos

4.1 Introduction

The vision of pervasive computing, the ability to access services and information anytime, anywhere, and from any device, is accelerated by emerging innovations in hardware, software, and network connectivity. Ubiquitous access presents an array of challenges, especially for applications in the mobile context because mobile devices have functional limitations due to size and available computational resources. Multimodal interfaces combined with careful considerations of the usability concerns in multimodal interaction can mitigate many of these limitations.

Recent efforts by technology companies and standards developing organizations [1, 2] underline the industry interest in multimodal interaction for mobile applications. In early 2002, Motorola and SpeechWorks announced the first prototype for distributed speech recognition and multimodal applications working over a deployed wireless network.[1] Around the same time, W3C proposed a new working group on multimodal interaction with the goal of extending the user interface of Web applications to allow multiple modes of interaction such as voice, keypad, keyboard, mouse, or stylus for input, and voice, audio, and graphics for output [1].

Multimodal interactions extend the Web user interface and offer a solution to the problem of data entry and access to information that is caused by the functional limitations of mobile devices. Single-mode interfaces exhibit inherent weaknesses; speech recognition is inaccurate due to the complexity of natural language, and the expressiveness of the graphical interface is affected by the size and resolution of the graphical display. As we move from a single-mode to mixed-mode interfaces and finally to multimodal applications, we can take advantage of the strengths of individual input and presentation modes in certain application scenarios and overcome their weaknesses by offering alternative modes of interaction. For example, users can choose to enter information by voice or with an input device such as keyboard or stylus; the output can be rendered through spoken prompts and audio or viewed

---

[1] http://www.motorola.com/mediacenter/news/detail/0,1958,1041_754_23,00.html

on graphical displays. Applications can be designed to combine multiple simultaneous input modalities and present information through synchronized rendering in multiple output channels. Multimodal interaction addresses the user experience challenges of mobility and ubiquitous access because it offers the choice of the appropriate combination of modes for each task, device, environment, and personal preference. Additionally, multimodal interfaces with supplementary modes of interaction improve accessibility for the elderly population and people with disabilities.

Multimodal interaction is a relatively new area in terms of mature development platforms and industry experience from deployed applications, but it is gaining momentum with several commercial tools in development and multimodal standards activities in progress. This chapter does not aim at providing a single methodology for authoring multimodal applications. Instead the goal is to highlight the main design principles when creating new applications with multimodal capabilities. It covers multimodal technology from the perspective of the application developer, starting with the underlying capabilities of the component technologies and a description of the currently available tools. It suggests a graphical syntax for documenting designs of multimodal applications, and discusses the main considerations that guide the development and testing processes. Lastly, we present a tutorial example that illustrates the design principles and highlights issues in writing multimodal applications.

4.2 Motivation: Multimodal Interaction Use Cases

Multimodal interaction enables users to communicate with a device in one or more input modes such as speech, pointing, writing, or gesturing, to express their intent and receive the output content in a combination of visual, aural, or haptic modes.

Generally, multimodal applications can be classified into one or more of the following categories:

- Form-filling
- Command and control
- Searching

The goal in form entry applications is to enter information in one or multiple fields and submit a form to a processing system in order to complete a transaction. A number of applications, such as access to a travel Web site or access to financial information, follow this interaction metaphor. Form-filling applications are primarily system-driven and impose a structured dialogue interaction. Multimodal interfaces for these applications merge graphical markup elements (e.g., HTML) or custom clients (e.g., J2ME) with voice. Typically, a user is offered the choice of which modality to use to provide data for each field in a form. These applications have a large number of grammars; the active grammar depends on the active field on the graphical view.

Command and control applications follow an interaction style where the user controls the application and the system responds to the user input. The command and control metaphor in multimodal applications provides supplementary graphical and voice interfaces for operations and offers the choice of modality to the user. These applications can be designed along the lines of a graphical menu, but this approach does not employ the full benefit of speech and natural language. An approach with richer user experience would allow the user to navigate naturally between different menus and provide "random access" to application functions.

The searching metaphor is related to applications that implement a mixed-initiative dialogue paradigm. Both the system and the user can take turns in controlling the flow of interaction. In addition to combining multiple input and output modes, a multimodal mixed-initiative application has rich dialog capabilities, and maintains the history of the interaction. Based on this history, it determines the optimal system response for the next turn or the appropriate help response to clarify incomplete input, correct potential errors, and guide the user through the application task. The benefits of mixed-initiative interaction are flexibility in switching between modalities and natural transitions between subdomains of the interaction.

The following use cases describe variations of multimodal interaction. The different modes of interactions are dictated by device constraints, user preferences, and environment constraints. Other factors such as network bandwidth, application, and service dependencies play an important role and should be considered in the design and implementation of multimodal applications as well.

4.2.1   Use Case 1: Multimodal Map

The user is carrying a mobile device with voice input/output capabilities and a touch-sensitive display that offers pen input for graphical navigation and handwriting input. The device is connected to a data network with high bandwidth and can also connect to other devices in the user's environment, such as the car.

The user is driving through the city and wants access to driving directions, points of interest, and restaurants using a multimodal map application that is connected to travel services over the network. While in the car, the application is accessible through the car console. The primary interface for input and output is voice with a very limited visual interface to limit driver distraction. The user points to the display while saying:

"How do I get there?"

The system combines the voice command with the location that was pointed on the map and displays the suggested driving directions as a graphics overlay on the map, and at the same time, uses voice output to give turn-by-turn directions to the driver. When walking through the city with the multimodal mobile device, the user can point to the display that shows a map of the area and ask for restaurants in the vicinity. The application can combine rich graphical information with voice output. At any time, the user can use a combination of modalities or switch to one of the available modalities, e.g., use the pen to draw a question mark for additional information or issue a command by writing.

Multimodal map applications are one of the most popular test cases for the study of multimodal interfaces. Researchers in the field have built several systems for travel planning to investigate issues such as simultaneous multimodal input, mutual disambiguation and error correction, and conduct usability studies [3, 4, 5, 6].

4.2.2   Use Case 2: Multimodal Voicemail with a Smartphone

The user starts the application either by dialing into their voicemail or selecting the voicemail icon from the graphical interface of the phone. The user issues a voice command:

"New messages"

The voicemail service responds with the voice output:

"You have three new messages"

and sends more detailed information back to the phone. A list of the three messages is displayed along with the time of the call and the caller ID information, if available. Depending on the capabilities of the device and the display resolution, the information can be rendered in graphics or in text. The user can interchangeably use voice commands, the keypad, or the stylus to navigate through the application selections, or to make a selection in a visual mode and issue a voice command; for example, the user selects one message from the list with the stylus and says, "Play." Similarly, the user can issue voice commands to navigate through the menus and receive confirmations or information in visual mode in addition to the standard voice output.

4.3   Discussion of Interaction Modes

In the field of Human Computer Interaction, a multitude of research and commercial systems have been proposed with diverse input and output devices and interaction modes [7, 8]. Graphical and voice interfaces, electronic gloves for three-dimension manipulation of objects, haptic and tactile feedback interfaces, and sensors to detect motion or acceleration have been employed to augment traditional application user interfaces and enhance interaction in areas such as consumer electronics, entertainment, training and education, and physical rehabilitation. In this chapter, we will focus our discussion on the graphical and voice modalities and their multimodal combinations for mobile devices. Figure 4.1 illustrates a generic framework for a system with multiple input and output modalities.

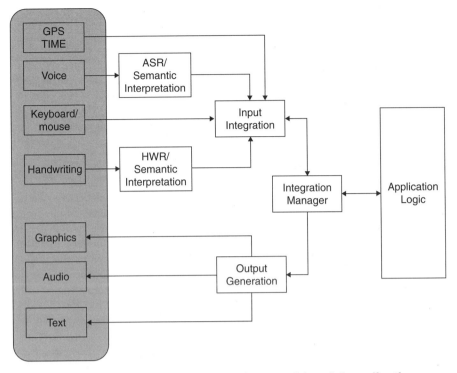

Figure 4.1   Generic framework for a multimodal application

4.3.1   Graphical User Interface

The graphical user interface (GUI), which was introduced by Xerox Palo Alto Research[2] in the 1970s, has become the prevailing interaction metaphor on desktops, personal digital assistants (PDAs), Web interfaces, and custom-built applications. In a traditional GUI environment, users provide input with the combination of the keyboard for entering text and the mouse for navigating the two-dimensional visualization on the display. Output information is presented visually in the form of menus, tables, and selectable items enhanced with images and animation. Additionally, part of the content may be presented aurally through sound and voice output. The GUI metaphor has remained fundamentally unchanged even though it has significantly evolved in terms of its user experience and number of features for additional functionality and improved aesthetics.

The Web browser, one of the most pervasive applications, is built around the GUI metaphor. The browser technology has advanced through standards, with markup languages such as HTML and XHTML, protocols such as HTTP, as well as

---

[2] http://www.webopedia.com/TERM/G/Graphical_User_Interface_GUI.html

Table 4.1   Input devices and modes for graphical user interface

Miniature keyboard	Text input
On-screen (soft) keyboard	Use of stylus or other pointing device for entering text
Stylus	Navigation, gesture, handwriting recognition, ink messaging
Numeric keypad	Text input with predictive text algorithms or multitap

commercial products that facilitate access to information and services on the World Wide Web (WWW) using the desktop computer. As wireless phones and PDAs with powerful hardware are introduced in the market – those that can support multimedia applications and have high-resolution color screens to display rich graphics content – the GUI-based browser becomes a viable way of interaction for ubiquitous information access with small mobile devices. Markup languages (e.g., WML and iMode) and protocols (e.g., WAP) were specifically designed to support access to content and services for small devices with limited computational power and low bandwidth cellular networks.

Mobile devices employ various communicative modes and users have become familiar with a number of different input devices for interaction such as the miniature keyboard and stylus. While we collectively refer to these devices and the corresponding modes as parts of the GUI, in the following table we identify the most common ones.

Devices with touch-sensitive displays have commonly used the stylus for navigation, while a variety of handwriting recognition methods [9] allow text input entered as a character at a time, whole words or phrases, or through the use of a special alphabet (Graffiti). The recognition task is based on probabilistic methods that are not error-free. The various approaches impose constraints on the permissible user input, such as accepting only letters, or symbols, or words. These constraints mitigate the complexity of the task and improve its accuracy at the expense of simplicity and naturalness for the user experience. Alternatively, these interfaces offer an on-screen (soft) keyboard where the user taps on the letters with the stylus in a hunt-and-peck mode. Many mobile devices can be connected to miniature keyboards that offer a compromise between mobility and the familiarity of the desktop keyboards. Finally, the numeric keypad on mobile phones has been proven an unlikely text input device as evident by the proliferation of SMS messaging. The combination of the numeric keypad with several proposed methods for predictive text input (iTAP, T-9) [10, 11] attempt to find a compromise between improving the speed of entering text while at the same time containing the user's cognitive load. A common characteristic is that input is converted to text but with the growth of the pen-enabled devices market, we are likely to witness applications that resemble the pen-paper metaphor where handwritten ink is the input – one such application can be ink instant messaging.

It is worth noting that the GUI in itself is a form of a multimodal user interface, as it combines multiple input devices (keyboard, stylus, display), multiple ways of providing input such as text and direct object manipulation, and it renders output in a variety of modes such as text, graphics, and audio. The visual interface represents information spatially, allowing the user to search visually for important elements of the content. In general, graphical interfaces excel at object manipulation and the point-and-click paradigm. Input entered via a visual/textual modality is flexible but tends to be slower, as the user must manipulate the input device. The input devices listed in Table 4.1 enable efficient text input for portable computing devices with limited resources and reduced form-factors but they become cumbersome, compared to voice interaction, for tasks that require lengthy inputs such as messaging and natural language interaction. In addition, visual interfaces based on mark-up languages are event driven and hence, they impose an implicit requirement that the user is familiar with the task and the expected input.

4.3.2 Voice User Interface

Voice has always been considered a natural medium for human-computer interaction and has motivated several decades of commercial and academic research in such topics as speech synthesis and speech recognition [12, 13, 14]. Early commercial systems were able to recognize a small vocabulary of words, whereas today's systems can recognize several hundred thousand words spoken by a diverse population of users with different dialects and speaking styles. Memory and computation requirements of speech recognition technologies depend on the complexity of the task, but they are typically high and create a dichotomy between thin client devices that connect to voice recognition servers and more powerful client devices with embedded speech recognition capabilities. The balance of satisfying the requirements of applications with limiting device capabilities leads to successful solutions that lie between these two extremes.

Two of the main drivers of growth for voice interactive applications are the need to access information content and services anywhere, anytime and the need for hands-busy and eyes-busy operation to ensure safety when driving a car or to increase productivity in enterprise applications. The wide availability of mobile phones has created new opportunities for voice interaction. Early voice recognition applications on mobile devices were primarily used for command and control or small vocabulary operations because of the device resource limitations.

The voice interactive applications, which use server-based voice recognition capabilities, were originally implemented using proprietary application programming interfaces (APIs). As the market for voice services grew, VoiceXML emerged as a standard for writing voice applications. VoiceXML [15, 16] is an XML-based language with declarative elements to represent dialogue-flow and grammars, as well as procedural elements to perform loops and conditional computations. This is a very powerful paradigm that offers high-level design constructs and flexibility to the application developer without requiring knowledge of the underlying details of the speech system. These details are abstracted in the high-level declarative features of the language. In addition, the acceptance of VoiceXML as a standard provides a degree of application portability across different speech server platforms. A number of companies provide access to VoiceXML implementations through Web interfaces; many can be accessed via the Internet and are easily located using Web search engines [17]. In contrast, the authoring of an application with an API approach requires a greater degree of specialized knowledge. The final application may gain in performance at the expense of losing portability to a different speech platform.

Although people use voice naturally for communication of complex, contextually sensitive information, voice interaction is surprisingly difficult for computers. For a voice application, a programmer typically writes a grammar that encompasses every possible valid utterance from a user. What would be a simple bank transaction for a person becomes an extremely detailed plan of events and grammars for a voice application developer. Voice applications require a more careful approach to programming since even a poorly worded prompt can severely damage the usability of an application. Voice interactions work well where a user must choose from a long list. Consider how long it takes to speak "Albuquerque" versus typing it (assuming one knows how to spell it) or locating it on a drop-down menu. But, voice is not a good medium for reading lists of results or receipt codes such as confirmation numbers, nor is it well suited to entering long strings of digits or character sequences. Consider that even a system that is 99 percent accurate on recognizing single digits will have an accuracy of only 90 percent for a string of ten digits. Is an application usable if it fails one in ten times? How long would you keep money in a bank that failed 10,000 transactions out of every million? As consumers, we've come to expect intelligent devices to "just work." But at the same time, we tolerate desktop computers whose operating systems and applications fail at an alarming rate. This creates a paradox for multimodal interfaces where reliable voice applications may mingle with less reliable Web technologies.

Input provided through speech comes quickly for humans; computers, however, are not adept with speech input. Whereas with a visual modality one must be able to spell, with a speech modality one must be able to pronounce. The same words that present problems for computers can be equally daunting for people. This is compounded by regional dialects, homophones, acronyms, and domain specific terminology. For example, the pronunciation of "route" can be R-OWT or R-OOT depending on the region of the speaker. Even simple combinations such as I-80 could be heard as EYE EIGHTY or I ATE "E". Although, improvements have been made, most applications will do well to limit the domain of their speech input.

Modalities are unidimensional; each addresses a limited interaction with a user and each has its strengths and weaknesses; these weaknesses lead to the benefits of combining modalities. Voice, visual, and graphical communicative modes are the most prominent and we largely focus on these in the rest of this chapter. Voice and graphical interfaces form a symbiotic fit, each overcoming the major weakness of the other. Where GUIs are more cumbersome for selecting from long lists, voice excels. And likewise, where voice is not suitable for rendering long lists or complex results, a GUI serves well.

4.4   Contextual Information as an Input Modality

Contextual information derived from location and time sensors, environment parameters such as noise levels and lighting conditions, and user preferences should be
considered when designing mobile applications [18]. For example, one of the benefits of a multimodal UI is that it can provide a combination of voice and GUI in a
generic setting, but when operated in a car, it can be used as a hands-/eyes-busy
voice only interface to ensure safety and reduce driver distraction. Similarly, multimodal applications would need to take into account accessibility requirements and
device profiles so that the application and interface adjust to the connecting device
characteristics. The design of a multimodal application could include information
from a sensor or a GPS receiver as a modality, or use the contextual information
received from a knowledge source to adapt the user interface.

4.5   Degrees of Multimodality

The previous use cases highlight different degrees of multimodal interaction with
respect to the use of the available input and output modes. Specifically, we can distinguish among:

Unimodal interaction: The application uses only one modality. Common
interactive voice services fit this category as do applications built in HTML or
WML.

Sequential multimodal interaction: The application can use multiple modalities but only one modality at a time is active for input. The active modality can
change in the next input turn. Modality switching may or may not be seamless; in
the latter case, transition between modalities are quite noticeable. A mobile application that initiates interaction in WML through a WAP browser and then suspends
or halts the WML to establish a voice connection will exhibit a potentially significant latency while the voice connection is established.

Simultaneous multimodal interaction: The application interface employs multiple input modes and can receive input from any one of them. The different inputs
are processed one at a time in the order that they were received, without any attempt
to combine them in a composite input.

Composite multimodal interaction: The application interface employs multiple input modes and can receive input from any one or a combination of more than
one of them. Based on a set of grouping criteria, the system can combine the individual inputs into a composite input that represent the user's intent. In this case, the
user can tap on the selection with the stylus and say, "Give me directions for this
one." The system is able to associate "this" of the verbal command with the object
of the deictic function of the stylus. In a classic example, a user speaks "from here
to there" while using a graphical touch pad to indicate points on a map at the same
time "here" and "there" are spoken.

We should also mention "SMS multimodality," a form of multimodal interaction that leverages short messaging (SMS and MMS) as a visual vehicle for
exchanging information. In the multimodal voicemail use case, the service can

respond to the initial query by sending a text message to the phone with the voice-mail information and the user can use the displayed information to advance the conversation with the service. This paradigm has significant potential because handsets are capable of receiving SMS messages during a voice session, and there is a huge deployed base of SMS-capable handsets.

These distinctions are important, not just to developers, but to network providers and ultimately, to customers. The usability of composite multimodal applications may far exceed the user experience of a sequential multimodal application, but at substantial cost. All of these degrees are possible with modern technology; however, sequential multimodal applications can also be made to work with older devices. The right degree to pursue may depend on the demographics of the customer base, the utility of the application, and the cost of the multimodal device.

The future of multimodal interactions will not be limited to single devices; indeed, many of the early experiments with multiple modalities used multiple devices, each representing a single modality. Surprisingly, this highlights some facts about the underlying networks: the voice and data networks (currently) are implemented as disparate networks that must be forced to interoperate. Protocols exist to mitigate this circumstance (e.g., H.323) but they are not widely deployed. The most successful experiments have been those where the voice and data networks are conjoined, which gives advantages to the application servers by putting both voice and data modalities under immediate control. When separated, the application program must make individual requests for each modality.

One of the challenges in the domain of multimodal interaction is aimed squarely at the application developers and application designers. As with other technologies, we strive to create rich and useful applications but at the same time, it is possible to create poor applications that leave a user wondering what to do next, what to say, and when to say it. This is partly dictated by the capabilities of the platform, but even more so, it is the result of suboptimal design. A usable application is possible even with disparate voice and data networks.

4.6   Multimodal Synchronization: What Makes Multimodality Work?

The design of multimodal applications needs to balance the temporal characteristics of voice interaction with the spatial nature of visual interaction. The defining feature of the multimodal experience is synchronization between the actions of the different input and output modes [19]. Examples where synchronization is a significant factor are:

- In the multimodal map use case, a user points at a location on the map while asking for driving directions. The application needs to have the capability to combine the information from the two input channels into a single composite communication act.

• In the multimodal voicemail use case, the application takes advantage of the display capabilities to show the list of messages to the user and verbally suggest the permissible actions. In a purely voice interface, it would be cumbersome to render the same information. The success of the multimodal system depends on the synchronization of the output channels to render the complementary information.

Regardless of the degree of multimodality, input and output in an application must be consistent across modalities in order to avoid confusion on the part of the user. Consider two simple applications, one based on VoiceXML and one based on HTML. Each one interacts with the user and delivers a weather report to the user. Independently, the two are separate programs. However, if these interfaces can be synchronized and share a common underlying interaction state so that the user may provide input via a keypad and then hear the weather report, they form a multimodal application. This model is actually suitable for designing applications, at least initially.

The other main characteristic that contributes to the operation of multimodal applications is the speed of mode switching. Any noticeable delay in operation degrades the usability of an application. A sequential multimodal application may have a noticeable delay when switching modes, whereas simultaneous and composite multimodal applications offer a seamless integration. Any operation that takes longer than two seconds is likely to cause the user to notice.

Latency is a significant factor for usability of multimodal applications. The time it takes between stimulus and response can significantly degrade the utility of an application. Of course, this depends on the nature of the application and it is often governed by urgency of the need and the expectations of the user. For example, checking flight status is a casual operation if one is waiting for a flight to arrive, but a critical operation if one is trying to catch a flight before it departs. Even though network delays may be unpredictable and unavoidable, it is an important design feature to provide feedback to the user on the status of the interaction. Appropriate audio and visual notifications can inform about these delays and more generally, provide guidance to the user through the completion of complex tasks.

Lastly, the capabilities of the voice and data infrastructures dictate the features available to developers of multimodal applications. A desktop solution provides the most freedom and processing power to the developer, but tethers the user to the desktop keyboard and microphone. A server approach can liberate the user from being bound to the keyboard by providing access to services through cell phones. This resolves the issue of mobility (if it is an issue), but the 2G cell phones have not been designed for this purpose and are limited in their ability to establish both voice and data communications simultaneously. The next solution is likely to build on advanced cell phones and networks with 3G capabilities; when implemented, 3G can support simultaneous voice and data connections. However, a situation can still arise where a system built on a 3G infrastructure can fail to provide a multimodal experience. For example, the GPRS network provides simultaneous voice and data connections in a class A network for a class A device. If the user roams to a class C network, the class A device will fall back to utilize only class C capabilities, which do not include simultaneous voice and data. Suddenly, from a user's perspective, their multimodal applications no longer work.

Although synchronization is at the core of the multimodal experience, numerous other factors contribute to that experience. Balancing the needs of the user with the capabilities of the technology is a key design element.

4.7   Solutions for Voice and Graphical Interfaces

Recent work on multimodal interfaces focuses primarily on the combination of voice, graphics, and visual modes. The creation of applications will benefit from open standards that facilitate the integration of multiple modes and the authoring of natural dialog interactions. Among the solutions that have been proposed in standards developing organizations, we highlight two specifications: XHTML+ VoiceXML and SALT. Although these solutions have similar objectives, namely to extend existing markup languages so that they support multimodal interaction, they achieve these objectives in different ways. Table 4.2 characterizes the similarities and differences of these solutions with respect to the individual modalities, whether or not they can easily incorporate new modalities beyond graphical and voice modes, and which modality plays the dominant role in controlling an application.

Speech Application Language Tags (SALT) [20, 21] is the result of a joint initiative, known as the SALT forum, created by Cisco, Comverse, Intel, Microsoft, Philips, and SpeechWorks. The SALT specification was submitted for consideration to the W3C Voice and Multimodal working groups in 2000. SALT adds voice capabilities to Web pages by defining a new set of tags to include in HTML pages. These tags provide a lightweight layer of abstraction for providing speech synthesis and speech recognition capabilities to existing markup languages. The SALT specification extends the syntax of HTML, making it easier to work with existing tools, but it suffers from the same syntactical shortcomings as HTML, namely, it is not regular and therefore, it is difficult to validate syntactically. The SALT solution provides the ability to control input for a single field so the developer can write their own code for managing input to many fields. This functionality is technically referred to as the Form Interpretation Algorithm (FIA). Direct support for additional modalities is

Table 4.2   Voice and graphical interface solutions

Solution	Voice solution	Graphical solution	FIA	Other modes	Dominant modality
SALT	New SALT tags	HTML	User writes	Yes, through scripting	Graphical
XHTML + VoiceXML	VoiceXML	XHTML	Provided	Yes, through markup	Graphical

not evident in SALT; while it is technically feasible, the developer is left to invent their own means for managing events with additional modalities.

The XHTML + VoiceXML [22] specification, known as X+V for short, was proposed by IBM and builds on two existing standards, XHTML and VoiceXML. Utilizing the existing VoiceXML standard gives this solution access to years of research and development that are incorporated into the VoiceXML 1.1 standard and paves the way for adopting future industry voice standards (e.g., VoiceXML 2.0). The use of the standard XML events provides a framework for handling event propagation in the XML tags. By virtue of using the XHTML document as a container, different input modes can be accommodated as modules. Currently, the X+V proposal uses the VoiceXML capabilities for the dialog and voice interface in combination with the XHTML that specifies the graphical content. Similarly, one can define a markup module for other modes such as handwriting input and touch.

Note that both solutions use the graphical modality as the dominant mode; that is, the graphical markup is the container for other modes. The reverse is equally possible and perhaps more natural because voice applications tend to operate under stricter constraints. For example, the graphical modality in a form entry application allows the user to choose the order in which items are filled; in a voice equivalent, the developer typically drives the order in which input is collected through a series of prompt-and-collect cycles. In such an application scenario, it may be easier to complement voice with graphics than it is to add voice to graphics.

These solutions are relatively new, having emerged in 2001. Both SALT and VoiceXML tags are relatively easy to learn, so the syntax of either should not be a hindrance. The XML nature of X+V is advantageous since even a single mismatch in tags in SALT can produce unexpected results, but, syntactic checking could be performed on SALT programs as well. SALT requires more programming for managing fields and implementing the dialog flow, while X+V builds on the VoiceXML dialog capabilities. Considering the relative recent emergence of these technologies and the early stage of the multimodal application space, it is far too early to determine how these two markup languages will evolve. For now, application developers will benefit from being familiar with both technologies. Microsoft provides access to the SALT markup through its .NET environment that is available for trial use. IBM provides trial use of its X+V multimodal browser through Internet Explorer and the Opera browser.

The degree of multimodality that is provided by these solutions depends more on the capabilities of the underlying platform than it does on the specifications. One could imagine an implementation for X+V or SALT that enforced sequential input by "muting" the graphical modality when speech is activated. But, equally feasible is an implementation that allows each modality to run independently and thus enables composite multimodal input. Numerous experiments with 2G cell phones yielded mixed results in trying to implement even sequential multimodal applications. On some cell phones, a mode switch from WML to voice would work as designed while on other cell phones, the same application would fail to switch modes.

4.8   Design of Multimodal Applications for Mobile Devices

Human communication is inherently multimodal: we communicate naturally and convey information with a combination of spoken language and gestures. The information in these separate communication channels is at times complementary and requires a composition of the separate sensory inputs in order to produce a complete semantic act. At other times, the combination of gestures and speech may be less critical to the meaning of the interaction, such as when providing emphasis. In designing a multimodal application, the focus should be on creating an efficient and effective interaction that follows the paradigm of natural human-human communication. The goals of a multimodal interface design should be [23]:

- Enabling faster task completion with less work.
- doing the right thing at the right time, tailoring the content and form of interaction to the context of the user, task, dialog, and environment

A successful multimodal interaction is one that accomplishes these goals and it is in this sense that it provides a natural interface to the device and the application. This is best described in the quotation by D.A. Norman [24]: "The real problem with the interface is that it is an interface. Interfaces get in the way. I don't want to focus my energies on an interface. I want to focus on the job."

In many respects, multimodal applications are no different from unimodal applications. A multimodal design process introduces a number of new aspects that need consideration but it is still founded on the principles and best practices of user-centered design. The development process collects requirements, generates suitable designs for each mode, and goes through an iterative cycle of review, development, and testing before delivering an application. The following sections highlight areas of development that require new attention in the realm of multimodal interfaces. In particular, we examine two areas:

- The audience and deployment environment
- The programming and design context

In addition, we briefly touch on two topics that are often overlooked during early stages of application development:

- Usability
- Internationalization and localization

These topics are very closely coupled with the details of individual modalities and have a significant impact on the human factors of multimodal applications.

4.8.1   Design for the Audience

As stated, design principles for multimodal applications are not new. They are a re-application of existing patterns within a new context [25]. The most significant parameter is the characterization of the user population. The audience for a multimodal application includes anyone with a cell phone (or other small communication device). Although some applications could be designed for use with a desktop computer (such as multimodal tax preparation software), we expect the majority of multimodal applications to target mobile devices because multimodality is inherently related to communication and mobility.

Understanding the needs of the target customers is paramount to the success of applications, a point that is amplified in the multimodal domain. Mobile applications must operate in hands-busy/eyes-busy environments and address the accessibility needs of people with disabilities. Traditional GUI interfaces assume that the user can see and operate a keyboard or other input device. Multimodal technologies create opportunities for supplementary modes of interaction that address these accessibility constraints. The application should be designed to operate with multiple modalities independently and gracefully reduce its functionality and features in the absence of additional interaction modes. By augmenting GUI interfaces with speech, visually impaired users would gain easier access to applications. It is worth noting that this approach is consistent with guidelines of the US government requiring equal access to government services and forms for all citizens [26].

4.8.2 Social Implications of Multimodal Interfaces

Although agnostic of any particular social concerns, the development of multimodal applications has the potential to enable new segments of users. More natural and flexible interfaces can reduce or remove barriers from members of society with disabilities and for those who are illiterate. At the same time, they pose new engineering challenges to their developers. For an interface available to the general public, what should the default modality be? If a blind person attempts to use an application that defaults to a graphical modality, how can that person switch to a voice modality?

Similarly, as the population of the world continues to diversify, multilingual interfaces will become more common. Switching languages for a multimodal solution can be tricky if the architecture does not support multiple languages simultaneously. This was a limitation in early voice interfaces that is now being surmounted. In short, knowledge about the users of an application will dictate many of its requirements.

4.8.3 Design for Context

Developers are accustomed to creating Web applications for specific servers and specific Web browsers. With multimodality, the potential number of deployed devices increases greatly. A user may have a home PC, one or more cell phones, and a PDA, all with different capabilities and unique characteristics; all of these (and more) are potential devices for multimodal interaction. Cross-platform interoperability can be facilitated by open standards, but the ability to cleanly separate application logic from device logic will be the critical factor for successful multimodal applications in this environment. This can be addressed succinctly in the design wisdom stated by David Parnas in the early 70s, "separate modules for separate concerns." [27]

4.8.4   Separation of Concerns

Regardless of the number and type of modalities, it is typically beneficial to design each modality independently at first and then merge them. The reason is that currently there is no prevailing and suitable public standard in place for multimodal application design. Separating along modalities divides the application along lines of expertise. Graphical designers may not have the skills necessary to create a suitable voice experience and likewise, a voice designer may not possess suitable graphical abilities.

Overall, the following separation can be applied to multimodal applications (Figure 4.2):

*   Core logic
*   Graphical interface
*   Graphical glue
*   Voice interface
*   Voice glue

Designing each modality separately would naturally lead to two (or more) implementations of the application logic. Identifying a separate application logic module is important because it creates a clean separation between interface and application back-end. More important though, creating common application logic shared by multiple modalities is a significant principle for multimodal design because it ensures that the various modes of interaction share a common interaction state. The common interaction state maintains the dialog history and the context of the communication between the user and the application, and facilitates the synchronization and consistency across modalities. More specifically, when the user switches modalities or changes dialog state, the application logic will ensure that a common context propagates to the interface so that the user can view and listen to the same content and interact with this content in any of the available input modalities.

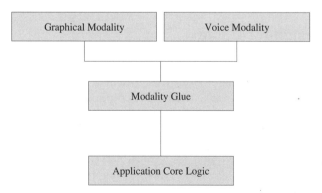

Figure 4.2   Separation of concerns for multimodal applications

Further consideration leads to the separation of the display logic from the rest of the system. This is a well-known approach to removing application logic from presentation, allowing the two to separately evolve. These types of modules contain the modalities presentation. A similar separation is performed on the input modalities.

The glue is a thin layer between the core logic and the presentation. The glue adapts the interaction between the core logic and presentation layers to a specific modality. In some cases, it may not be present or it may simply be present as part of the controlling modality. Most often, the glue is the code that propagates events or data between modalities. Figure 4.2 illustrates this organization.

An example of this glue is used in MXML to link graphical events to the voice interaction. Applications designed in this manner are easier to implement and maintain. These concepts are further illustrated in the tutorial example.

4.9 Internationalization and Localization

Internationalization and localization have been guiding principles for the design of graphical applications and voice applications independently. These features are required for the design of multimodal applications in order to ensure correct operation in different geographic regions. Multilingual interfaces are often addressed by removing string references to resource or property files. This approach also works with multimodal applications, but implementers often make erroneous assumptions about the ability to substitute and concatenate strings to form proper sentences in different languages.

4.10 Usability

Usability is an often-overlooked aspect of graphical applications. The confluence of multiple communication channels creates new challenges for the usability of multimodal interfaces. The visual modality is capable of displaying a variety of information simultaneously. In contrast, a voice interface can only present a single stream of information at a time to a user. From a design point of view, the two modalities can complement each other and the successful combination would aim to address their individual limitations.

Still, at times conflicts will arise. Consider a graphical application that first queries the user for a name in order to personalize the user experience. The equivalent operation in voice would let the user say his or her name, record the result, and then play back the user's original voice as needed. But how would this interface fare in the multimodal realm? A grammar of all names and pronunciations may provide some help but inevitably cannot account for variations in spelling, such as distinguishing "Lori" from "Laurie." Admittedly, this is somewhat contrived since a voice application typically queries a user for an account number or some other unique identifier, and then references the user's name from a database. A set of questions to help illuminate potential problems follows:

- How is navigation performed (e.g., between "pages")?
- How is focus selected in each modality?
- How is a button activated?
- How are drop-menus activated? Do they graphically respond to voice?
- How are radio lists and check boxes selected?
- What does "barge-in" mean on a graphical interface?
- What is the overall look-and-feel-and-sound of the application?
- How to design appropriate voice prompts and matching visual elements in order to avoid confusion and at the same time draw the correct response from the user?
- How to transfer control of the interface from one modality to another in a seamless way that does not disrupt the flow of the application and is apparent to the user?
- How to maintain the dialog state between interaction turns that may involve modality switching? (Modality switching may be dictated by environment constraints or user preferences)
- How to adjust the interface to address privacy and security concerns of the user?

This is not a mandatory set, but rather a selection of the types of questions that should be asked during the design process. The set of questions to consider varies, depending on the application and its intended users.

4.11 Design Artifacts

In this section we present a straightforward approach to designing a multimodal application. During design, this approach combines graphical and voice designs into a single unified view, ensuring that that designers are aware of all modalities and concerns. The flow is divided into "fields" and "forms" that are roughly equivalent to fields on a form in VoiceXML. This "field" view gives the ability to focus on a single slice of behavior of the application while the "form" view shows the flow between elements. The design notation for "fields" is summarized in Figure 4.3.

The set of events that are part of the design is determined by the modalities employed. For voice modalities, the set maps to those supplied by VoiceXML such as "NO INPUT #," "CANCEL," "HELP," and so on. The graphical input events are from the graphical host environment, HTML or XHTML for SALT and X + V, respectively. They include such events as "FILLED," "LOST FOCUS," "GAINED FOCUS," and so on.

The field view, as previously noted, shows a single input field in the system along with all of its input events and potential state transitions.

The form view shows all the field items and how they connect with others. It also shows elements such as background grammars and other design notes. For a multimodal Web site, related fields should be grouped into separate forms.

Note that this notation does not address any aspect of the actual graphical layout, as it is a design notation and not an implementation. Further observe, this design approach combines the modalities into a single view; alternatively, they can be easily split into separate views, developed independently, and then later com-

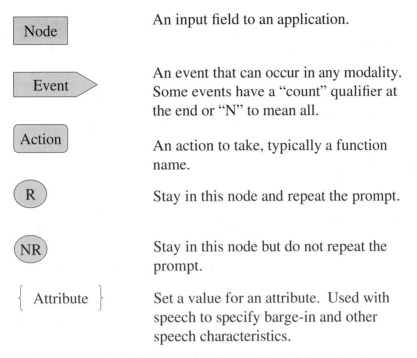

Figure 4.3   A design notation for multimodal applications

bined. Lastly, keep in mind that a design notation serves its users, not the other way around. Architects and engineers should embellish as needed to effectively convey their designs.

4.12   Testing Multimodal Applications

Multimodal programs are an order of magnitude more complex that single modality applications; the greater the number of modalities, the greater the complexity. This is not surprising since the number of possible input combinations explodes combinatorially. The most straightforward strategy for testing is to test each modality separately and then test them together. It should be clear that because of the multimodal interactions, the testing effort for multimodal applications will be greater than the sum of testing each modality independently.

The testing evaluation needs to follow a design process that identifies the proper flow of control, and the available interaction options along with their value in user experience (e.g., are the modalities providing composite input or serial input etc). Objective performance metrics can be established in the form of task completion rate, time required to complete a task, ease of use, and learnability of the new interface. Lastly, usability testing with representative user populations will provide preference metrics and insights about the features of the system.

4.12.1   Testing Strategies for Multimodal Designs

Multimodal applications offer new possibilities for interaction between man and machine. They also offer new sources of failures and frustrations. Just as design patterns need reinterpretation for multimodal, so do the strategies for testing. Two strategies that are most applicable to multimodal applications are:

- Requirements based
- Failure mode analysis

Naturally, the requirements for an application must be tested – this is a given. Failure mode analysis and testing gives the bullet-proofing needed for a commercial application to ensure that the user experience is not compromised. The set of failure tests should also include those undesired events such as equipment and network failures, as well as actions that are outside the scope of the expected inputs. For example, many users today try to "zero-out" of IVR services by pressing and holding the zero key on the keypad.

As previously discussed, it is often beneficial to develop each modality separately, test them, and then merge them. This isolates the complexity to a single modality at a time until the final application is ready. It also provides a natural separation for development. Once the separate modalities are operating correctly, multimodal testing can begin. The design and implementation of a test harness will need to verify the functionality of the graphical and voice modalities, as well as their multimodal combinations in interactions such as: "From here, [click] to there [click]". An automated scripted process would be best suited to test the very large number of execution paths in a multimodal interface. Some of the fundamental test cases are outlined below:

- Mode switches – For usability, this is one of the most critical aspects of multimodal. Mode switches must be clean and robust.
- Loss of each mode – Consider a sequential multimodal application with a graphic and voice modality implemented on existing systems using VoiceXML and WML. Handoffs between modalities are performed using the respective URLs for each language, coupled with session management on each server to retain appropriate state information. But what if one of these servers fails, or fails to respond in time? Where does that leave the user? Or consider a GPRS network where the user is on the fringe of the network, where they keep dropping and reconnecting.
- Half-inputs from a mode ("half an utterance") – Depending on how the grammar is written, it may be possible to fill in only part of a form with an utterance. When multiple slots can be filled, thoroughly test combinations of partial information.
- Conflicting input from modes – What response would an application generate if the user provides conflicting inputs? Since two events will not have the exact same arrival time, which one will take precedence? What would a user expect?
- Network performance and latency – How long it takes to switch modes in sequential multimodal applications will always be an issue. Network latencies for remote data based applications will impact performance as well. Voice can

travel over a data network using Voice over IP (VoIP) and distributed speech recognition (DSR) technologies (as demonstrated by the Motorola prototype), but what are the bandwidth limitations?

This is not an exhaustive set but it demonstrates the line of thinking that should occur in the testing realm.

4.12.2 Multimodal Testing Environments

Evaluating the resulting application in conditions that simulate the deployment environment is certainly a desirable and required stage in the development process. Still, a number of helpful evaluations ca be accomplished before planning for a broad test over the wireless network and the target hardware. The basic approach for a testing facility closely matches the various degrees of multimodality.

Unimodal applications require no special equipment, and there are already abundant test facilities for graphical and voice modalities that run on a programmer's desktop or in a lab environment.

Sequential multimodal applications that include gross modality switches can likely be tested using existing facilities as well. Testing strategies for this class of applications would examine the operation of each modality independently using desktop simulators, and then test the mode switches using the target hardware equipment.

Simultaneous and composite multimodal applications offer new challenges for testing. There are not yet testing platforms for simulating anaphoric inputs (e.g., "from here to there"). A likely first approach is to construct scripted tests that simulate the conditions of the target environment, taking into account characteristics such as latency and network reliability.

4.13 Tutorial Example: Designing and Implementing a Multimodal Color Chooser

To illustrate the concepts put forth for design and implementation, we consider a tutorial example with a sample implementation in both IBM's MXML environment and with SALT. The example is a multimodal Web page that allows a user to create a background color by specifying the red, green, and blue components of a color. The tutorial presents the top-level designs for the graphical and voice flows, and a sample implementation.

Program Statement: A multimodal application using graphics and voice that allows a user to set red, green, and blue values for a background color.

Figure 4.4 shows the "form" design using the notation described previously. The design is quite simple: once the page loads, the focus is set on a command field and the user is prompted visually through static text and audibly through the voice interface. After each command, the screen is updated with any changes and then the user is returned to the command prompt. The design notes indicate that there are not

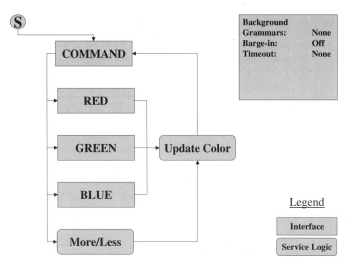

Figure 4.4   A flow design for the multimodal color chooser

any background grammars and that by default, barge-in is not active. This simple diagram captures only the most abstract interaction between fields and forms.

Figure 4.5 shows the details for obtaining the red component. Following the design, implicitly, the user is prompted to enter the value; the prompt is specified as well. If either text input is provided through the GUI, or the user speaks a match for the grammar, then the color is adjusted and the application returns to the *Command* node. The other events handle the less desirable cases; where the user does not speak a match, he or she is prompted again. If the user has not spoken, he or she remains in the same node but the prompt is not replayed. If the user says, "cancel," the value is cleared and the application proceeds to the *Command* node.

An implementation for this design using MXML is shown in following sections. Although contained in a single Web page, the source is logically structured to separate the voice and graphical elements, enhancing the readability and main-tainability of the code. The exception is the voice GUI glue that associates each graphical form element with its voice form element; for clarity, these are juxtaposed. The structure of the program follows the design patterns previously discussed and is divided into the following sections:

• Program logic
• Voice interface
• Graphical interface plus voice glue

The program logic section contains a set of JavaScript functions that are actually the core of the program's functionality; everything else in the program is dedicated to the interface logic for the modalities. The voice interface consists of a set of forms that mirror the fields of the graphical interface. They are named simi-larly, after the color that they represent. Lastly, the graphical portion contains stan-dard XHTML markup, plus the code to link to the voice interface.

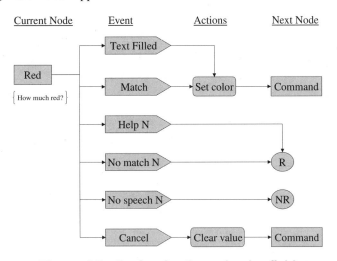

Figure 4.5   Design for the red color field

The VoiceXML for this example is not difficult to program: it uses all standard and well documented VoiceXML constructs. The `form id` "red_quantity" is used later to uniquely identify this dialog so that it can be activated when the red field receives focus. The field name "rquantity" is completely internal to the VoiceXML and is used only to store the results from the speaker's utterance. The grammar for this field (and the green and blue fields as well) is stored in a file in JSGF format. All three fields share the same grammar source file, so only one copy is needed. The `<vxml:catch>` statement is the error handling catch-all. The only magic in the script is the command in the `<vxml:assign>` block which transfers the value collected through the voice interface into the form element's value.

For simplicity, the red voice field above is mimicked for the green and blue colors; a more advanced approach would take advantage of VoiceXML subdialog facilities.

The graphical elements are even simpler than the voice elements; they are standard HTML with the addition of a few attributes that link them to their voice counterparts. The name of field provided in the `form id` attribute, as previously demonstrated, is used by the voice interface to transmit the results from the voice modality to the core program logic.

The `ev:event` and `ev:handler` attributes work together to activate the voice dialog for this field when it receives focus. All of the other attributes are standard HTML attributes. The next line, the `ev:listener` tag, instructs the browser on how to handle the completion of the voice modality on the "redQuantity" field. Here it invokes a function in JavaScript to process the results.

Together the voice and graphical elements form an interface shown in Figure 4.8. Note the addition of a set of buttons that perform the same functions as the voice commands. These were added for debugging the program logic independently of the voice interface. Essentially, this made it possible to "unit test" the program's

```
<vxml:form id="red_quantity">
  <vxml:field name="rquantity">
  <vxml:prompt>How much red?</vxml:prompt>
    <vxml:grammar src="digits.jsgf" />
    <vxml:catch event="help nomatch noinput">
      Say a number between one and two hundred fifty five.
    </vxml:catch>
    <vxml:filled>
      <vxml:assign
          name="document.getElementById('redQuantity').value" expr="rquantity" />
    </vxml:filled>
  </vxml:field>
</vxml:form>
```

Figure 4.6   VoiceXml dialog for the red color

```
<input type="text" value="150" id="redQuantity"
    ev:event="focus" ev:handler="#red_quantity"/>
<ev:listener ev:event="vxmldone"
    ev:handler="#handleQuantityDone"
    ev:observer="redQuantity" ev:propagate="stop" />
```

Figure 4.7   The graphical element for the red color

Figure 4.8   A screen snapshot of the multimodal color chooser

Table 4.3 Testing results

Modality	Test	Description
Graphical	Edit color	Click on red, green, and blue in turn and change their values. The background color should change appropriately.
Graphical	Zero color	Click on red, green, and blue in turn and enter zero for the value. The screen should become black.
Graphical	Max color	Click on red, green, and blue in turn and enter 255 for the value. The screen should become white.
Graphical	Negative color	Set each value to −1 and to −255 in turn. Negative values should be rejected upon input.
Voice	Edit colors	Use the voice commands to test more, less, and change for each color, red, green, and blue. Observe the results and document any cases that fail.
Graphical and voice	Interaction	Select change for a color. Provide simultaneous input through both modalities.
Voice	Stuck PTT	Hold the speech activation key for a duration of 60 seconds.
Graphical and voice	Boundary	Enter and speak values larger than 255 for each color.
Graphical and voice	Input type	Enter and speak non-numeric characters for each color.
Voice	Digit type	Speak a large value (253) as individual digits (two-five-three) and as a number (two-hundred-fifty-three).

Note: The granularity of these tests is quite large. In a production environment, each test would likely be broken down into a number of subtests. Also note that our first implementation will not pass all of the listed tests, namely the rejection of negative and large numbers.

operation so that when the voice interface was tested, aberrant behavior would be attributed to the interface logic, not to the program logic.

Testing our sample program follows the strategy for sequential multimodal applications. Separate tests are used for each modality to establish their operation independently. Table 4.3 below summarizes the tests:

We purposefully kept the tutorial example simple and focused on showing a slice of the development cycle. The example can serve as a starting point for the interested reader. A set of proposed changes is listed below; for each of the changes, start by modifying the design documentation before changing the implementation.

- Provide a means for the user to edit the "step" variable that controls how much color is added or removed when it is changed.
- Convert the program to use hexadecimal instead of RGB.
- Extend program interface to accept user preference for entering either hexadecimal or decimal values for RGB values.
- Refactor the program to use a single subdialog that is shared for each color.
- Redesign the program to allow the user to say all three color elements in a single utterance.

4.13.1 Using SALT

So far the example has used IBM's Multimodal Extensions (MXML) for the implementation; this section illustrates how to use SALT for the same program. The SALT environment is provided by Microsoft and can be downloaded from their Web site. Note that SALT requires specific versions of IIS, MSIE, and their .NET framework. The SALT SDK can integrate with the Microsoft .NET Studio, but this is not required to try out the tools. This section highlights only the conversion of the MXML example into SALT. A complete code example is contained in following sections.

Moving from MXML to SALT highlights that the early emphasis on a solid design was not wasted. All of the service logic of our sample program is completely reusable. Additionally, the graphical elements can all be reused with little modification; only the speech tags must be completely replaced, plus some additional scripting is needed to tie the SALT tags together. Moving from one system to another is also beneficial, as it highlights the differences between the two technologies.

SALT, like MXML, follows an approach of building on existing technologies by allowing a user to map the results of speech to JavaScript elements that are subsequently used to drive program logic. Binding to speech events is performed using Microsoft extensions to the HTML events. Consider the input field for the red color, in SALT, a first attempt might use the "onclick" event to link in the voice tags; however, this would require changes to the service logic as well, since it sets the focus in response to commands. A better approach is to use the "onfocus" event as shown here;

The speech events are handled through attributes of the `<salt:listen>` tag, most notably, `onReco`. This provides a convenient means to invoke a JavaScript method to handle the results of the recognition. The specified `<salt:bind>` tag maps the results of the recognition into the HTML field.

Repeating this modification for all of the other input fields gives us a suitable mechanism for activating the voice modality when a field receives focus. It also provides a grammar for the speech modality and copies the results into the input element's value.

One element is missing for the input fields, which is the set of prompts. Prompts are provided in SALT by using the `prompt` element shown below for the three colors.

```
<input type="text" value="150" id="redQuantity" onfocus= "red_quantity.Start()"/>

<salt:listen id="red_quantity" onReco="doCommand('show me')">
    <salt:grammar src="digits.grxml"/>
    <salt:bind targetElement="redQuantity"  value="//num"/>
</salt:listen>
```

Figure 4.9   SALT version of graphical and voice code for red

```
<salt:prompt id="red_prompt">How much red?</salt:prompt>
<salt:prompt id="green_prompt">How much green?</salt:prompt>
<salt:prompt id="blue_prompt">How much blue?</salt:prompt>
```

Figure 4.10   SALT prompts for the colors

```
<input type="text" value="150" id="redQuantity"
    onfocus= "red_prompt.Start(); red_quantity.Start();()"/>

    <salt:listen id="red_quantity" onReco="doCommand('show me')">
        <salt:grammar src="digits.grxml"/>
        <salt:bind targetElement="redQuantity"  value="//num"/>
    </salt:listen>
```

Figure 4.11   Final version of red color in SALT

To add the prompts in, we can modify our input fields to invoke JavaScript to provide the standard prompt and collect behavior. The new version is shown here:

Converting the input fields and prompts as above completes the transformation and the application is now available as a SALT application. Note that in SALT, there is not an explicit form statement for grouping elements akin to the dialog and subdialog tag in VoiceXML. In its place, the programmer writes additional code to link fields. To illustrate the needed changes, consider modifying the program to allow the user to say all three color values in a single utterance; for example, the user might say "25 30 35" to populate the fields for red, green, and blue, respectively. In addition to modifying the grammar to accept the three values, the programmer might also – for example – add the following logic to the program:

This provides a rudimentary form interpretation algorithm modeled from the examples provided with .NET Studio, where the programmer manually specifies the prompt and collects actions and invokes the script repeatedly to ensure that all fields are filled. Additional code is needed to invoke the script at the appropriate times to collect the values.

The last part of the example that needs to be converted is the grammars. MXML used the JSGF format. SALT employs the speech recognition Grammar Specification (SRGS), a candidate W3C recommendation. The grammar conversions are in the appendices along with the complete code example.

The example demonstrates that multimodal applications are a reality and that both SALT and MXML are capable platforms for creating and testing multimodal

```
<script>
function myFIA()
{
        if (redQuantity.value="") {
            red_prompt.Start();
            red_quantity.Start();
        } else if (greenQuantity.value="") {
            green_prompt.Start();
            green_quantity.Start();
        } else if (blueQuantity.value="") {
            blue_prompt.Start();
            blue_quantity.Start();
        }
}
</script>
```

Figure 4.12   SALT code to support filling multiple fields

applications. Switching from one system to another brings out the real message for any multimodal effort: invest in a solid design. This is the best way to insulate programming effort from dependencies on the technologies, especially at this natal stage of multimodal technology and standards.

4.14   Summary

Multimodal is a revolutionary approach to application design that brings man and machine interaction closer than ever before. It has the potential to remove barriers that limit unimodal interactions, creating a new era of interaction. Although true multimodal applications are not yet mainstream, the technology needed to produce them has now arrived and it is only a matter of time before our phones, computers, and other devices employ interfaces that conduct a natural conversation, with the user utilizing visual and verbal modes.

For application designers, it should also be clear that the bar has been raised. The effort required to design, implement, and test a multimodal application is larger than implementing multiple applications in each modality. A new set of issues arises in the interactions between the modalities, but these issues can be addressed using careful design and thorough testing practices.

Tools for experimenting with multimodal technologies have been around as long as the terminology: WML, HTML, and VoiceXML provide one suite of markup languages that can be combined into a multimodal platform. Other approaches favor creating new markup languages or avoiding markup altogether.

Two markup language specifications are published at this date: SALT and XHTML+Voice. The SALT approach extends HTML and integrates with Microsoft's .NET environment. It provides a good solution for simple voice interactions but can require significant programming effort for complex interactions. The .NET environment provides a graphical interface to designing SALT based applications. The XHTML+Voice approach builds on numerous XML standards including XHTML and VoiceXML. Because VoiceXML is a full-fledged voice application system in its own right, it provides a more suitable solution when the voice interface is larger and more complex. Prudent technologists will acquire expertise with both solutions – and with other forthcoming solutions – in order to ensure that they are able to choose the appropriate technology for each solution.

Regardless of the chosen technology, by their very existence, it is clear that the age of multimodal interfaces has now arrived in force.

4.15   References

1. World Wide Web Consortium (W3C), Multimodal Interaction Activity http://www.w3.org/2002/mmi/.
2. Open Mobile Alliance, http://www.openmobilealliance.org/.
3. Cheyer, A., and Julia, L. (1995) Multimodal maps: An agent-based approach. In Proceedings of CMC95, Amsterdam, 1995, 103–113.
4. Johnston, M., Bangalore, S., and Vasireddy, G. (2001). MATCH: Multimodal Access to City Help. In Proceedings of ASRU 2001 Workshop, Madonna di Campiglio, Italy.
5. Almeida, L., Amdal, I., Beires, N., Boualem, M., Boves, L., den Os E., et al. (2002). Implementing and evaluating a multimodal and multilingual tourist guide. In Proceedings International CLASS workshop on natural, intelligent and effective interaction in Multimodal dialog system, Copenhagen, Denmark, June 2002.
6. Oviatt, S.L. (2000). Multimodal system processing in mobile environments. In Proceedings of the User Interface Software Technology Conference, Nov. 2000, San Diego, CA.
7. Oviatt, S.L. (2003). Multimodal interfaces. In The Human-Computer Interaction Handbook: Fundamentals, Evolving Technologies and Emerging Applications, (ed. by J. Jacko and A. Sears), Lawrence Erlbaum Assoc., Mahwah, NJ, 2003, chap.14, 286–304.
8. Oviatt, S.L. (1999). Ten Myths of Multimodal Interaction, Communications of the ACM, 1999.
9. Seni, G., and Subrahmonia, J. (2001). Pen-Based user Interfaces – An Applications Overview. In The Computer Engineering Handbook, Oklobdzija V (ed), Series Electrical Engineering Handbook, vol.25, 2001.
10. Motorola, Lexicus Division. iTap. http://www.motorola.com/lexicus/html/itap.html.
11. Tegic Communications. T9. http://www.tegic.com/.
12. Srinivasan, S., and Brown, E., (2002). Is Speech Recognition Becoming Mainstream? IEEE Computer Magazine, April 2002, 38–41.
13. Padmanabhan, M., and Picheny, M. (2002). Large-Vocabulary Speech Recognition Algorithms. IEEE Computer Magazine, April 2002, 42–50.
14. Gorin, A.L., Abella, X.X., Alonso, T., Riccardi, G., and Wright, J.H. (2002). Automated Natural Spoken Dialog, IEEE Computer Magazine, April 2002, 51–56.

15. World Wide Web Consortium (W3C), Voice Browser Activity, http://www.w3.org/Voice/.
16. VoiceXML Forum, http://www.voicexmlforum.org/.
17. Ken Rehor's World of VoiceXML, http://www.kenrehor.com/voicexml/.
18. Lum, W.Y., and Lau, F.C.M. (2002). A Context-Aware Decision Engine for Content Adaptation. In IEEE, Pervasive Computing, July–September, 2002, vol.1, No.3, p. 41–49.
19. Oviatt, S., De Angeli, A., and Kuhn, K. (1997). Integration and synchronization of input modes during multimodal human-computer interaction. In Proceedings of the workshop Referring Phenomena in a Multimedia Context and their Computational Treatment, ACL/EACL'97, July 11, 1997, Madrid.
20. SALT Forum, http://www.saltforum.org/.
21. Tang, S. Adding SALT to HTML, XML.com, May, 2003, http://www.xml.com/pub/a/2003/05/14/salt.html.
22. IBM Pervasive Computing Software, Multimodal Toolkit and documentation, http://www-3.ibm.com/software/pervasive/multimodal/.
23. Maybury, M. (2001). Coordination and Fusion in Multimodal Interaction. MITRE, Technical Report, November 2001.
24. Norman, D.A. (1990). Why interfaces don't work. In Laurel B (ed) The art of human-computer interface design, 1990, p. 209–219.
25. Weiss, D., and Hoffman, D. (eds) (2001). Software Fundamentals: Collected Papers by David L. Parnas.
26. US Department of Justice A Guide to Disability Rights Laws, May 2002, http://www.usdoj.gov/crt/ada/cguide.htm.
27. Parnas, D.L. (1972). On the Criteria to Be Used in Decomposing Systems into Modules. Communications of the ACM, December 1972, vol.15, No.12, p. 1053–105.

Chapter 5

Heuristics for Designing
Mobile Applications

Roman G. Longoria, Mick McGee, Eric Nash

5.1 Introduction

With mobile devices and wireless infrastructures becoming more powerful and ubiquitous, the corporate world is striving to use these technologies to keep their businesses competitive. One way is to provide access to enterprise applications via wireless, mobile devices. Designing mobile enterprise applications provides unique challenges. The obvious challenge is to design for small devices and usage in a mobile context; however, you may also need to design for integration with desktop products, novice users as well as domain experts, and a scalability of functionality that usually exceeds traditional consumer-oriented mobile applications and services. This chapter discusses enterprise mobile application design heuristics derived from iterative usability cycles that yielded a wealth of ideas and validation data. Although this chapter focuses on enterprise applications, many of these heuristics can be applied to more consumer-oriented applications.

The next section briefly summarizes the design heuristics for quick reference. This is followed by more detailed explanations.

5.2 Summary of the Heuristics

1. There is a need. It is clear that there is a need for enterprise level mobile applications. Spend the resources to conduct thorough interviews and task analyses with existing and potential customers so that you can understand the use cases and design for the specific mobile context.

2. Every pixel counts. Although this sounds like an obvious comment, it is meant to emphasize the need to rethink traditional screen layout principles when designing for mobile devices. Maximize the use of the available screen display.

3. Every round trip counts. There is a fine line between the need to keep pages simple and the need to put enough information on the page to decrease the number of round trips to the server. While it may be perfectly acceptable to access

key information by drilling through several pages within a desktop application, this may quickly become intolerable if the user must wait several seconds to download each page within a mobile application.

4. Employ "feature shedding." Don't try to shove a desktop application into a mobile device. You should not try to map a desktop application's hierarchy or full feature set into the mobile application. Although you may be used to thinking of what types of features you can add to your software product, when designing mobile applications, it is just as important to consider those features you should leave out.

5. Keep your navigation model simple. While this heuristic persists regardless of whether a mobile or desktop application is being designed, the need is greater when designing mobile applications. Stringent limitations in screen size, memory, network transmission, and user input methods commensurately place limits on the content of the pages of the application, as well as the number of pages that should appear, and how they should follow from one another.

6. Think modular. Creating modular, "plug-in" functionality will allow you to provide added value to applications when contextually appropriate. For any application designed, the pages should follow one another in a seamless and coordinated fashion. The first step in achieving this is to design the elements within a mobile application with a standardized set of visual characteristics and interaction rules. Such standards should encompass the essential elements you plan to use within your mobile applications.

7. Minimize data entry. No matter how much the user input technology improves for mobile devices, the need for data input will continue to annoy users. Beyond technology used to aid data entry, simple interface designs can be used to limit the need to type or otherwise enter information into a PDA or Web-enabled phone. For example, use "selection" over "entry."

8. Allow for desktop-based customization. Leave the heavy lifting to the desktop. The key to successfully designing a mobile application is mapping the functionality and information within it to the users' mobile contexts. Obviously, getting this right for every user for every mobile context is a difficult goal to attain. A method you may want to employ is to provide a sufficiently rich set of features, but allow end users to customize their unique experience with the application based on their unique mobile contexts, personal preferences, and corporate data.

9. Fight the hype. It is important not to get caught up in any particular hot mobile technology, for it is likely to change over time. Focus on those core attributes of the technology that seem more stable. Although it may not be wise to get too caught up in the specifics of the devices, you should be aware of them, for they are more likely to impact immediate design decisions.

10. Basic UI principles still apply. All devices are not reincarnations of the PC. Therefore, UI lessons learned for the PC need to be adapted for the mobile form factor. However, basics UI principles and methodologies still apply.

5.3 Heuristics in Detail

5.3.1 Heuristic 1: There Is a Need

Through interviews with existing and potential customers, it is clear that there is a need for enterprise level mobile applications. The mobile workforce is a reality. For Enterprise Resource Planning (ERP), Customer Relationship Management (CRM), and Business Intelligence Systems (BIS), customers have a vested interest in accessing key functionality and information in order to accomplish critical tasks in the mobile context.

There are numerous trends that indicate the world's population, and its workforce, is becoming more and more mobile. Anticipating and preparing for these trends will leave your company and products well poised to take advantage of these eventualities. Now the key challenge is smartly positioning your company to follow the right trends and not be so far ahead of today's realities that no track record of success can be established. That's why it is imperative to understand these trends and the use cases today's mobile workers find themselves in.

One of the more salient and easily measurable trends is the sale of cell phones and other associated mobile devices. The growth of cell phone sales has increased exponentially. The latest prediction is that there will soon be a billion cell phones on the planet. That number may not be reached given the recent economic climate and stability of the telecom industry, however, anything close to a billion is a *lot* of mobile devices already being carried around by users everywhere. It would be naïve to say cell phones have not added to modern culture and dramatically changed communication.

Beyond cell phones, the PDA industry was previously limited mostly to custom-built industrial devices. Today, it may seem like everyone has a PDA. And pagers, formerly the most ubiquitous enterprise mobile device, are now relegated to second-class status despite being the second most common mobile device in terms of quantity sold.

Along with the Web, all this improved communication has helped lead a second trend, the globalization of modern business. Many other business resources can be researched on this issue. However, it is clear that in the last century, far more borders were opened to outside influences than were closed. Recognition of the world as a global customer has led more and more businesses to expand not only their sales to other countries, but their workforces as well. Furthermore, much of the Middle East and Asia is poised to rapidly jump into the modern age with their huge populations and maturing industrialized nations. The support structure for this enormous global workforce will include, by default, more travel, more mobility, and more communication across a wide array of connectivity devices.

All of the devices mentioned thus far are the salient ones that people carry around and actively use. There is another coming wave of technology that will transform currently-passive devices into nodes in a ubiquitous computing world. This communication ability will increase the usefulness and possibilities for mobile devices. "Ubiquitous computing" is a vague phrase for the notion that communicating computing devices will be embedded into all sorts of common everyday items (walls, elevators, refrigerators, clothes, jewelry, and more). The networks (e.g., Bluetooth, WiFi) will take advantage of this ubiquitous computing environment to make mobility and mobile devices an even more integral part of our lives than they are today. Companies had better be prepared to invest the necessary resources to identify where they and their products will fit in this mobile world.

Examining the Mobile Context

Before extending our minds fully into the wilderness of the future, understanding the current basis of the mobile user is essential to preparing for success in this domain. A fundamental principle that must be understood is that nearly any primary computing task can be more efficiently accomplished over a faster network connection with larger viewing and input areas than with mobile devices (e.g., the typical desktop PC). Therefore, mobile contexts are centered on situations where that access is not available, either by design or coincidentally. The two main mobile contexts for the enterprise worker are:

1. Employees whose primary work is conducted away from an office (sales, service, and so on).
2. Business professionals whose primary work is within an office, but are temporarily away from their desks (or any PC network connection to the virtual office).

The field worker is an important enterprise application user. Whether the user is a sales representative working primarily on the road, a service worker primarily working at a customer site, or any other worker who primarily works outside an office, the main access to data is through a mobile application. The frequency with which the users in this context interact with the mobile application may be higher and the information and functionality provided may be a more integral aspect of their jobs.

The "normal" business professional operates mainly out of an office with a fast, large computing connection. However, there are endless opportunities for owners of mobile devices to fill their otherwise daily unproductive time with secondary access to everyday business applications. The more common usage contexts include users who may be: 1) traveling in another geographical location; 2) commuting within their hometown locale; 3) waiting for a meeting to start (or in a boring one), standing in line, or otherwise in a relative state of inactivity; and/or, 4) simply choosing to access a network through a simpler connection than their PC.

These applications accessed in this "secondary" mode may be mainline business applications associated with their work (database management, finance, and so on) or they may be accessing business applications (such as email, calendar, or file sharing). In both cases, mobile use is secondary to main data access points (e.g., a PC in an office), a vast myriad of usage scenarios may be encountered, and a more "get in, get out" design approach may be warranted.

Beyond the main breakdown of user types, there are several general mobile usage characteristics that need to be considered for any mobile user: 1) mixed environmental conditions, 2) multitasking, 3) intermittent interaction, and 4) social engagement.

There is almost no environmental condition in which a mobile device cannot be used. Certainly there are network coverage limitations, however, asynchronous functionality (i.e., that which does not require a network connection because the data is stored on the device) can compensate. Whether the environment is bright, dark, rainy, windy, bumpy, smooth, fast, slow, day, night, quiet, or loud, the possibilities are as endless as the earth (and space) is broad and ever changing. Designing for all possibilities is impossible. Understanding the appropriate environments for your product is critical.

One aspect of mobile applications and their context of use is *multitasking*. Although perhaps we need to consider multitasking as more of a continuum, as multiple concurrent tasks are possible even within four cubicle walls. It is better to conceptualize the possibilities of multitasking in the mobile context as being much more prevalent and potentially complex, even dangerous. It is hard to avoid reported debates on cell phone use and driving. In fact, many communities are considering laws to ban such activity altogether. More mundane multitasking involves socially interacting while using a PDA, or attending a meeting and using a PDA.

Depending on the mobile context, and possible multitasking, *intermittent interaction* needs to be considered as a high likelihood rather than an unusual occurrence. Intermittent interaction in mobile use can be much more frequent and short-lived than with a PC, where going to lunch or shutting down a machine at the end of a day is "intermittent." A mobile user may be simultaneously hailing a taxi, engaging in conversation with an employee, or as mentioned previously, focusing on a primary task like driving, and responding to that context of use and secondarily operating a mobile device.

Many of these tasks are undertaken at the same time because a mobile user is often interested only in retrieving a very select piece of information relevant to his or her current situation or thought process. This is the "get in, get out" phenomenon of mobile use for anything other than the most dedicated mobile user.

Lastly, integral to many other usage situations, *social interaction* is much more likely during mobile computing than in other more sedentary computing environments. Even chatting in Internet "rooms" with live interaction is done from the privacy of a nodal Internet connection. Web cafes bring people together, but again, usually as independent islands rather than socially interacting crowds. Mobile devices are computing devices that can be brought to the social environment, immersing use in situations that have very little to do with the application itself.

The many possibilities of social interaction is yet another layer of complexity to consider when designing mobile applications. For example, do users typically avoid crowds to use their mobile device? Do they carry them in bags or purses? Are they in pockets? Do they use them to communicate with family? Is it socially acceptable to talk loudly in plain view of strangers? What are the security risks in social environments? Is style a consideration? Depending on your product, these considerations may take primary importance, but cannot be ignored in any design situation as they are unavoidable.

Of course most mobile applications are specifically designed to function in specific contexts, the main one discussed here is the enterprise user. Most enterprise users will not be chasing tornados in the US Midwest or using their enterprise applications at a bar. Perhaps the most likely variable conditions the enterprise user will encounter will be those of the business traveler. The business traveler extends the needs of the secondary business application access with a need to deal with an unknown location. Access to local information becomes an additional need (e.g., driving directions, train schedules, nearest ATM, local entertainment guides, and so on).

The scale of the challenge associated with mobile design described above makes understanding the context of use one of the preeminent tasks for any mobile designer. The assumptions of desktop use cannot adequately dictate mobile use scenarios. This nature of mobile use has complexities that only a few designers have begun to consider.

5.3.2   Heuristic 2: Every Pixel Counts

As mentioned earlier, one obvious hardware constraint that hinders the usability and utility of mobile applications, is that the screen size to display and interact with information is very small. The usable display area varies within and between device types, so at Oracle, we have developed device type specific estimates (in pixels) for safe design heuristics (see Figure 5.1). For standard Web-enabled phones, a typical width is around 96 pixels (or 12 characters). The height depends on how many lines the phone has. Our heuristic is basically 8 pixels in height per display line (e.g., 3 lines = 24 pixels, 6 lines = 48 pixels). Personal digital assistants (PDAs) also vary in screen size. For the Palm^{TM}, we still design for 153×144. For Windows Pocket PC devices, we design for 240×268. For horizontally oriented "smart phones," basically a combination of phones and PDAs, we design for 240×120. Compare these numbers to typical desktop or Web applications designed for either 1024×768 or 800×600.

Obviously, no matter the device, every pixel counts, and all effort is made to maximize the available display area. This heuristic emphasizes the need to rethink traditional screen layout principles when designing mobile applications for PDAs or Web-enabled phones.

The critical balance between a clean layout and presenting data to the user results in rethinking how data are presented. This can be illustrated in three commonly used page types in enterprise applications:

- Label-data display pages
- Tabular display pages
- Form pages

Each of these page types will be discussed in turn.

Label-Data Display Pages
Label-data pages are those which display an object's attributes in read-only format. Traditionally, these types of pages display text in a two-column, page centered format, with the labels right aligned in one column and the data left aligned in another. This leaves the white space outside of the text. See Figure 5.2, Option A. However, this layout is an inefficient use of space in that too much white space is created. Compare Figure 5.2 Option A with that of Option B, which left aligns the

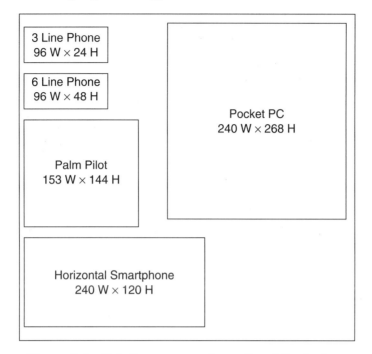

Figure 5.1   Relative screen sizes of mobile devices

A

B

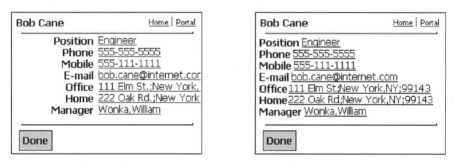

Figure 5.2   Layout options for a PDA application

entire page and separates the label and data with one non-breaking space. Our usability data indicated that users were just as fast at scanning the page and finding data with this format, and got the benefits of being able to read more data. Another approach is to use the two-column format, but reduce the width of the first column to the character width of the longest label; however, this approach loses its benefits as the labels increase to eight characters or above.

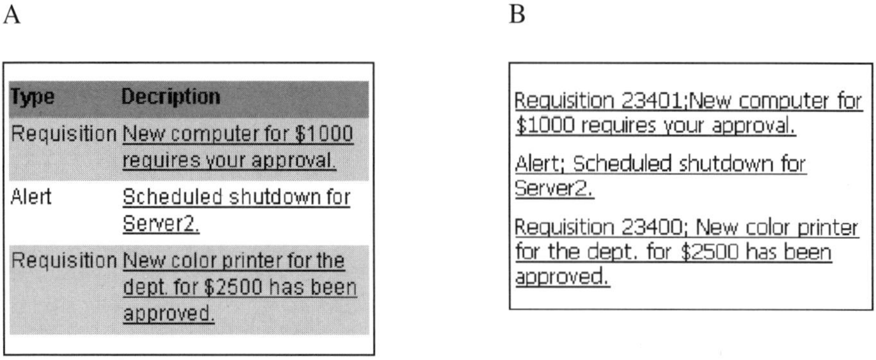

A   B

Type	Decription
Requisition	New computer for $1000 requires your approval.
Alert	Scheduled shutdown for Server2.
Requisition	New color printer for the dept. for $2500 has been approved.

Requisition 23401;New computer for $1000 requires your approval.

Alert; Scheduled shutdown for Server2.

Requisition 23400; New color printer for the dept. for $2500 has been approved.

Figure 5.3   Table layout option with concatenated data

Tabular Display Pages

Another method of making the best use of available display area is deciding when to use tables for presenting data. For example, instead of showing data in tabular format, concatenating the columnar data into a single string saves space and has only a minor impact on visual scanning speed, especially when combined with putting the key differential data at the beginning of the string. See Figure 5.3. Option A shows data presented in a traditional two column tabular format. Option B shows the same data displayed with the data concatenated and separated with semicolons. With Option B, you can show the same amount of data, using less space. By concatenating, you can save vertical real estate, thereby increasing the amount you can display and reducing the amount of vertical scrolling.

Concatenating column data is preferred when:

- You can read the data as a single object
- Data in one or more columns is presented in long text strings
- The user is not often comparing data from one row to another

It can be expected that the user will want to visually scan data in one or more columns (e.g., for comparisons or for adding). Concatenating column data (Figure 5.4, Option B) does make it difficult for users to compare across rows as compared with a true tabular format (Figure 5.4, Option A). Icons for alerts are displayed for specific units of data. Concatenating the column data in this scenario would make it difficult for users to perceive the alert icons.

A   B

Figure 5.4   Table layout option with tabular formatting

A   B

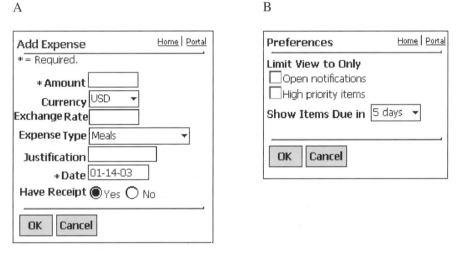

Figure 5.5   Layouts for form pages

Form Pages

Form pages are those in which the user enters or updates data. Traditionally, these types of pages display text in a two-column, page centered format, with the labels right aligned in one column and the form controls (e.g., text boxes, drop down lists, radio buttons) left aligned in another. This leaves the white space outside of the text. See Figure 5.5, Option A.

Our usability data indicates that this is still the preferred layout in most cases. The main exception, as shown in Figure 5.5, Option B, is when labels are exceedingly long, and a centered page format would cause horizontal scrolling. In this case, it is better to left align the labels and place their corresponding form controls below them.

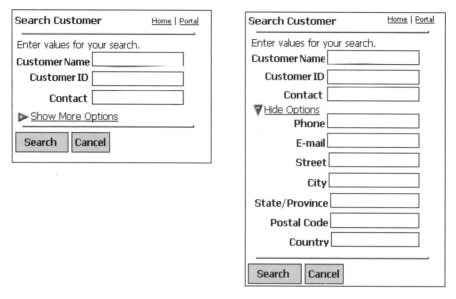

Figure 5.6   Use of progressive disclosure

Use of Progressive Disclosure

Progressive disclosure refers to the concept of surfacing the most important information or functionality to the user, while still allowing for the less critical or frequently used to be discovered. This has the benefits of taking enough display area to show which is most frequently used, as well as reducing the download time of a given page. In Figure 5.6, progressive disclosure is used in a form page, which displays the most frequently used form controls, with a link to "Show More Options." Clicking this refreshes the page and displays more form controls. The benefit of using this type of model is that the user would not normally need to perform any vertical page scrolling to initiate the search by tapping on the Search button. A heuristic we have used to justify this type of progressive disclosure is when there are four or more additional search criteria that are not expected to be used often (20 percent of the time). Otherwise, we put all of the search criteria on a single page.

The type of progressive disclosure shown in Figure 5.6 should not be used for the following scenarios:

- Content that a user must see, and is crucial to completing a task should not be hidden.
- Required information that can be updated should not be placed in a hidden area.

In some cases, it may be useful for the system to remember the state of the hidden or shown area. If a user has shown a section of content on a page, then leaves the page, the section of content shown should still be visible when the user returns.

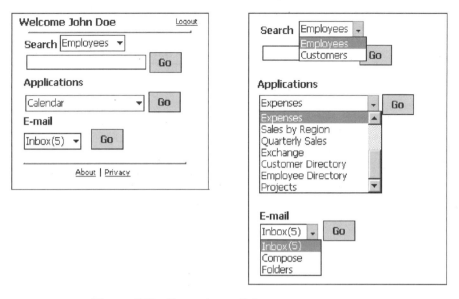

Figure 5.7   Drop-down lists can save space

Using Drop-Down Lists to Save Space

The creative use of drop-down lists is another effective technique to maximize display area. In some cases, flat lists can be avoided. This is beneficial as they are inefficient both in terms of display area and navigation. Drop-down lists can surface key information and functionality, take up less space, and save round trips. Figure 5.7 illustrates how drop-down lists can be used to present a full range of search, application, and email choices without the need for any scrolling.

Another use of drop-down lists we have employed is in substitution for the need to exceed one row of buttons. Typically, buttons are used to initiate an action; however, only a few buttons can be displayed on a single row. Having multiple rows of buttons has been problematic for users in usability testing when only the first row is visible. This is because users typically think they have reached the end of a page when they see a row of buttons and do not expect that they need to scroll down to view more buttons. See Figure 5.8.

5.3.3   Heuristic 3: Every Round Trip Counts

When deciding what content to assign to a page within a mobile application, a balance must be struck between omitting enough content to keep pages simplistic and surfacing enough content to minimize the number of round trips to the server. Minimizing round trips to the server is crucial to the design of mobile applications when considering the slower round trip times (RTT) of today's wireless technology relative to desktop technologies. While it may be perfectly acceptable to access key information by drilling through several pages within a desktop application, this may

Preferred   Problematic

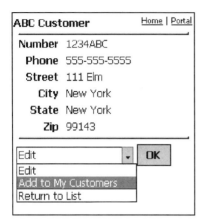

Figure 5.8   Using a drop-down list instead of stacking buttons

quickly become intolerable if users must wait several seconds to download each page within a mobile application. Until wireless technology can be improved, it is critical to surface key content quickly so that the number of additional pages that must be downloaded is minimized.

The term "content" within this topic is meant to include not only data, but also user interaction. As an example of the latter, consider the case where a user is expected to delete a target object frequently within a mobile application. As one alternative, the user first selects the target object by clicking a link, which navigates the user to a separate edit page. The edit page then allows the user to delete the object by clicking a page level "Delete" button (see Figure 5.9, Option A). The page content is simple and clear; however, it is also clear that deleting the object cannot occur without two server trips. The more this operation is expected to be performed, the greater the time loss required to download the second page. As an alternative, suppose both selection and deletion take place on the same page, using radio buttons to select the object and a page level button to perform the deletion (see Figure 5.9, Option B). While the page content is more cluttered and less clear, these disadvantages will likely only surface for the novice user, and will be offset by the savings gained by requiring a single server trip to complete the action.

This heuristic can be easily overlooked when page files viewed on an emulator or device are cached, saved locally, or used over an internal network because RTT is artificially reduced. As a consequence, design alternatives that may appear favorable during design reviews or usability testing conducted under the reduced RTT ultimately become less so when viewed within the actual RTT of a wireless network. Fortunately, several emulators and devices support simple client side scripts capable of delaying the presentation of page content so that wireless network RTT is better approximated.

Another manner in which you can save on round trips is by providing more information on a page that will give the user enough information to decide whether clicking on a link or otherwise navigating to another page is even necessary. In

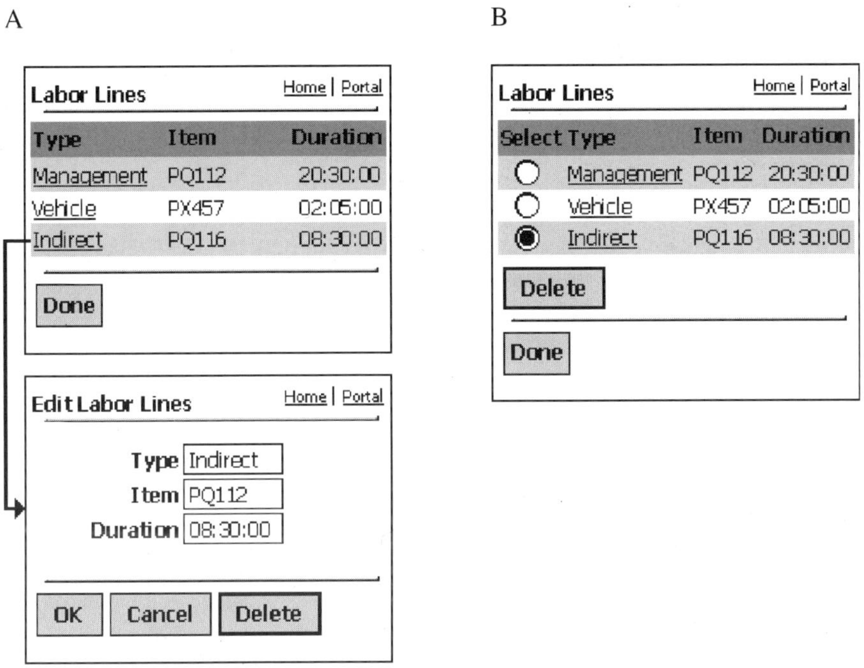

A   B

Figure 5.9   A method of reducing server round-trips

**Figure 5.10   Providing information
on whether navigating to another
page is necessary**

Figure 5.10, the Email drop-down list provides the user with the number of new
email messages. If this number reads zero, then the user would know that there is
no need to navigate to the Inbox.

 We have also found it useful to allow users to navigate directly to functionality within an application. In Figure 5.11, the Email drop-down list allows users to
directly navigate to either the Email Inbox, compose page, or folder list. This UI
mechanism eliminates the need for users to navigate to a more generic email
home page, from which they would need to perform further navigation to the desired
functionality.

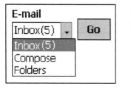

Figure 5.11   Allowing users to navigate directly to specific application functionality

Other technologies can be used to push some client side validation to the device. JavaScript and xForms may provide some of this, and thus reduce the need for the end user to pay the price of server side validation. However, not all devices support JavaScript and even fewer will support xForms any time soon.

5.3.4   Heuristic 4: Employ Feature Shedding

Don't try to shove a desktop application into a mobile device. You should not have to map a desktop application's hierarchy or full feature set into the mobile application. Although you may be used to thinking of what types of features you can add to your software product, it is just as important to consider those features that you should leave out when designing mobile applications. Remember that the mobile application should solve an immediate and critical need of the user. The trick is to find out what that need is and to ignore the rest.

This problem becomes increasingly important as the corporate world seeks to have its enterprise-level business software become "mobilized." Additional challenges arise in this case due to migrating the functionality of desktop or Web-based applications to mobile devices. Just what is the mobile context of your enterprise users? What assumptions can you make about the needs of the users in a mobile context? How much positive or negative learning transfer is there between desktop applications and mobile applications? These are all major questions that should be addressed in the design of mobile applications.

As the devices get smaller in form factor (seen here in Figure 5.12), decreasing from desktop to a voice application, the application should shed functionality so that only contextually appropriate features are provided to the user. This "feature shedding" is an essential, and perhaps the most difficult, part of mobile application design and development. The areas within each device type section represent the functionality that can be supported because of the device type's form factors. A desktop application can provide more functionality than a PDA, simply because there is more screen real estate and a more powerful processor, as well as other factors. As you design for smaller devices, and ultimately voice applications, focus on features and UI methods that are best suited for the device type. The most important features of a desktop application may not be the ones you would want to expose in a complimentary voice application.

Often it is the case that the navigation model for the desktop application was developed prior to designing the mobile application. While some of the more generic principles of moving forward, backward, and cancelling processes from a desktop navigation model can be applied to the mobile device, the limitations of the latter necessarily reduce any applied navigation model to solve an immediate and critical

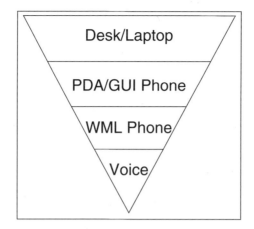

Figure 5.12   Feature shedding based on device form factor

need. Typically, the solution can be found within a subset of the functionality available in the desktop application. Choose the features from this subset and discard any features not directly contributing to solving the need. Deciding between the features to include and those to discard is possibly the single greatest difficulty in designing mobile applications. However, without doing so, mobile applications quickly become reduced in their effectiveness to accomplish their goals.

Once you have a distilled set of functions ready for mobilization, it is good practice to consider any circumstances that may impede users from using your mobile application. First, consider whether there are any existing alternatives for accomplishing the goal of your mobile application. If these alternatives exist, ask yourself whether the goal is more easily accomplished by your mobile application or the alternative. The obvious implication is that if the alternative is easier than the mobile application, there is little incentive for users to use the latter (especially since its feature set was intentionally reduced to address the goal). In this case, your chosen mobilized feature set may need revision to provide functionality not provided by the alternative, or the mobile application itself may not be needed.

While great pains might have been taken to define a narrowed feature set to mobilize from a desktop application, the complexity and/or security of the selected features is an additional impedance to whether the mobile application will actually get used. Mobilizing enterprise applications is particularly vulnerable to this impedance because individual features can often require a large number of actions, the disclosure of an abundance of information from various sources, or may govern information absolutely critical to the user. The more a selected feature is characterized by these, the less comfortable users will feel using it on a mobile device, and the more likely they are to utilize other means (such as the desktop application running on a laptop) to accomplish the goal. Therefore, in addition to choosing the feature set, ensure that users won't feel as though the mobile application's features and information disclosure are too risky to justify its utility. Attention to these points in developing a navigation model ensures the survivability of a mobile application.

5.3.5   Heuristic 5: Keep Your Navigation Model Simple and Clear

Defining the navigation model for any application determines what features users will use, how they will move among various pages, how the application will allow users to recover from errors, and how it will prevent users from getting lost. While these issues persist regardless of whether a mobile or desktop application is being designed, the need for simple solutions to these issues is greater when designing mobile applications. Stringent limitations in screen size, memory, network transmission, and user input methods commensurately place limits on not only the content of the pages of the application, but also the number of pages that should appear and how they should follow one another. This topic will explore means by which the navigation model can be simplified for mobile devices.

Provided that a reduced feature set has been chosen that meets the considerations previously discussed, it is important to consider how navigation should be organized within your mobile application. There are generally two distinct models that can be applied: detail-oriented and action-oriented. Detail-oriented models refer to applications where the user's primary objective is to obtain information (e.g., find a customer address or phone number). The goal of the navigation model should then be to surface the information to the user as quickly as possible. From here, it is likely that the user may want to do something with the information (e.g., call or get directions). The navigation model should therefore progressively disclose its functionality on the same page that the information is surfaced. Action-oriented models refer to applications where the user's primary objective is to perform one or more tasks (e.g., buy from a store or submit an expense report). The goal of the navigation model should then be to surface the features that can be performed as quickly as possible. In this manner, the user can more easily discover and perform a set of actions on an object without drilling into the details of the object.

Provided that decisions have been made regarding detail and action list navigation models, the navigational model can then begin to dictate the types of elements to include within the pages of the mobile application. For any page within the mobile application, it is important that no more than three to five navigation points be provided. Providing more than this can lead to unclear expectations for navigation and increases the chance that users will navigate to pages irrelevant to their tasks. Also, it is important that each page provide a set of universal anchors (e.g., "Home" or "Portal") that navigate the user to a consistent destination (see Figure 5.13). Such simplicity and consistency will result in users becoming quickly familiar with the

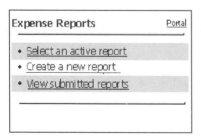

Figure 5.13   Using a universal navigation anchor

Figure 5.14 Use of a consistent "drill-up" method

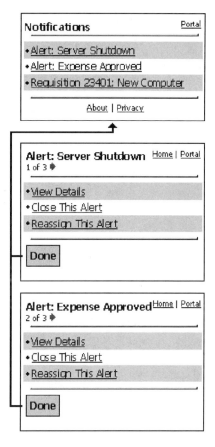

application and will increase the chances that users will be able to quickly navigate to a familiar point if they become lost or experience difficulties.

The navigation model will rely heavily on the application hierarchy. As such, a mobile application hierarchy should not exceed three to four vertical layers. Going beyond this will most likely require that the pages of the application provide some type of navigational cue, such as bread crumbs, to inform the user of the current location. While this practice commonly occurs within desktop applications containing complex information hierarchies, such cues come at a much higher cost to mobile devices because screen real estate is scarce. It is therefore a design compromise to limit the number of vertical layers of the application hierarchy so that any screen real estate that would be needed for the display of navigation cues can be assumed for purposes more relevant to satisfying the goals of the mobile device. In addition, when there is a potential for lateral navigation across a single vertical layer of the application hierarchy, having a constant element in place for "drilling-up" to the next highest layer (see Figure 5.14) will reduce reliance on the "hard" browser buttons for backward navigation, and will provide a clear and direct means for exiting any given layer within the hierarchy.

5.3.6   Heuristic 6: Think Modular

For any designed application, the pages should follow one another in a seamless and coordinated fashion. The first step in achieving this is to design the elements within a mobile application with a standardized set of visual characteristics and interaction rules. Such standards should encompass the essential elements you plan to use within your mobile applications. Using standard elements will not only provide a family of headings, labels, fonts, colors, and layouts that can be combined with flexibility across the pages of a mobile application, but also will improve consistency, simplicity, and minimize re-design.

As standard elements are combined to create each page, and the pages are in turn combined to create page flows, the benefits of modularity persist. Consequently, complete page flows and even full applications may be combined to reap the same benefits of flexibility, consistency, and simplicity outlined for combining standard elements. As a rudimentary example, suppose standard elements have been combined into a page flow for the purpose of sending text messages to other users (see Figure 5.15, Option A). While this particular page flow might be useful enough to stand alone as a complete mobile application, it is reasonable that such functionality might also be useful within other mobile contexts. For instance, suppose an additional application has been designed that allows a user to search for details on employees within the organization. After searching for the details on a particular employee, it would be useful to click the employee's email address to send a message. Hence, the message composition page flow could be integrated with the employee page flow. A modular architecture would allow you to do this in a way that is consistent and coordinated, with minimal redesign (see Figure 5.15, Option B).

It should also be mentioned that practicing design in this way is not without its share of disadvantages and potential pitfalls. Having just provided examples showing the advantages of modularity, it should be noted that just because page flows can be combined does not necessarily mean that they should be combined. Superfluous combining of page flows may clutter the mobile application to the point where the advantages of modularity are lost. This can be avoided by conducting a thorough analysis of the mobile context that identifies the appropriate functionalities to combine. Additionally, if the standards used to design for modularity are not already in place, creating, enforcing, and maintaining them can be difficult, especially within a large development organization. Lastly, once such standards are in place, design conflicts are often incurred when a new element or interaction that appears optimal cannot be applied because its function can already be assumed by a (less optimal) standard. While utilizing standards in this way can often result in feeling that a design has been compromised, the hope is that the benefit of consistency derived from the use of standard elements will outweigh any benefit from using the more optimal design.

5.3.7   Heuristic 7: Minimize Data Entry

No matter how much user input technology improves for mobile devices, excessive data input will continue to annoy users. There should be no disputing that mobile

A   B

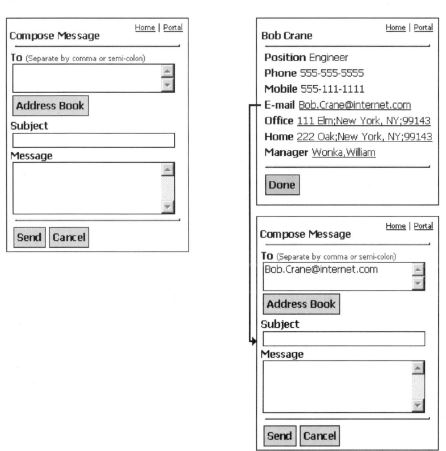

Figure 5.15   Modular use of email functionality

interfaces should, wherever possible, minimize all data entry. No mobile development project should begin with the assumption that the same amount of data manipulation can be performed on mobile devices as on complete desktop systems. This
is a common early thought for teams new to mobile development. It must be clearly
communicated that mobile applications should include convenient mechanisms that
alleviate the need for frequent data input. The reality is that not all applications
developed for mobile use will be able to eliminate all data entry. The challenge is
developing technologies and methods to minimize data entry in the most suitable
and acceptable fashion for all the respective mobile contexts.

        Several technologies specifically being developed to minimize the difficulty
of data entry are proliferating in the mobile domain. For PDAs, the use of handwriting recognition technology is meant to lessen the "pain" associated with data

Figure 5.16   "Pal" is input using T9 technology; each indicated button is pressed once

entry. Its success in this area has been mixed, as evidenced by the numerous "hard" and "soft" keyboards that make handwriting recognition unnecessary.

The huge numbers of existing cell phones with their small phone keypads has caused necessary innovation in data entry simplification along a different path than PDAs. However, in most cases, the methods used to simplify data entry on phones can be adopted by PDAs.

The most common data entry minimization technique for cell phones is text entry using predictive algorithms. T9 is one such method that attempts to computationally predict the word being typed based on the key combination of the numbers/letters pressed (see Figure 5.16). Typical cell phone data entry is called "multitap," where four presses of #7, for example, displays the text letter "s" (refer to #7 key in Figure 5.16). T9 claims input twice as fast as multitap.

Other text entry algorithmic methods attempt to guess what word is being typed based on the first few letter entries. These types of systems attempt to reference databases of word usage built from common sources (newspapers, magazines, books, and so on) to determine the most likely word wanted by the user. For example, "Ariz . . . = Arizona." Some systems even incorporate contextual information from the surrounding words and sentence to estimate the most probable word being typed.

Selection Instead of Entry

Beyond technology used to aid data entry, simple interface designs can be used to limit the need to type or otherwise enter information into a PDA. Radio buttons, check boxes, list boxes, drop-down lists, or simple lists of links can all be used instead of data entry. The programming challenge is simply to develop sensible lists of options that can reasonably be used by these UI mechanisms. This can be accomplished by either "system" defined defaults, or "user" defined defaults. "System" defined defaults for a list may include keeping track of the most recently used selections, with the assumption that they are the most likely candidates for future use. "User" defined defaults for a list may include those the end user customizes (e.g, "My Customers," "My Locations").

5.3.8   Heuristic 8: Allow for Desktop-Based Customization

As mentioned several times before, the key to successfully designing a mobile application is mapping the functionality and information within it to the users' mobile contexts. Obviously, getting this right for every user for every mobile context is a difficult goal to attain.

A method you may want to employ is to provide a sufficiently rich set of features, but allow end users to customize their unique experiences with the application based on their unique mobile contexts, personal preferences, and corporate data. The predefined lists, searches, or preset text strings can quickly be used in some mobile interaction sequence. Furthermore, certain functionality can be "hidden" (i.e., not displayed on the mobile device) if a user does not frequently access them.

Often this level of customization can be too cumbersome for accomplishing on a mobile device. We recommend that for all but the simplest customizations, the user be directed to a desktop or Web application. While users expect enterprise mobile applications to be ready-to-use, they do request some level of customization, and really do not want to do heavy duty work from the device itself.

5.3.9   Heuristic 9: Fight the Hype

It is important not to get caught up in any particular hot mobile technology. This can be a device, application, or any layer of the technology stack (for example, the gateway, service provider, manufacturer, or programming standard). The technological specifics of the mobile domain are certain to change over time. In fact, they have already changed very rapidly over the last 5–10 years with the adoption of digital telephony networks. Focus on those core attributes of mobile technology that seem more stable.

Of course, one cannot focus exclusively on a "stable" technology in the mobile domain. While a track record of success needs to be established with the current technologies that are available now, products need to maintain flexibility to incorporate important new technological developments as they become available if they are to stay relevant and viable. Any large-scale mobile development effort needs to carefully consider this balance. Are the latest advances important and useful for the intended (or existing) platform? Are they easily assimilated, or is the advance significant enough for a change to the platform itself? These are far from trivial questions.

There are basically two schools of thought on which wireless mobile devices (and subsequent underlying technologies) are used to access a company's enterprise mobile applications. Either the individual company is going to dictate which devices are going to be allowed, or the framework will allow access to any mobile device with a wireless connection. It seems unreasonable that many large companies would dictate specific device usage (at least for wireless connectivity). So if you are focusing on a potentially broad spectrum of devices, you may wish to focus design efforts on those with the largest market share.

The specifics of the devices, however, are likely to change over time. Again, focus on those attributes of the device that seem more stable. For example, the pixel size of the display area is probably less stable as a device property compared to the markup language used to deliver applications to that device. Also, stylus input appears to be here to stay in one format or another, as well as the general form factor of PDA layout. However, the exact size and peripheral interaction mechanisms are likely to vary from one manufacturer to the next.

Although it may not be wise to get too caught up in the specifics of the devices, you should be aware of them, for they are more likely to impact immediate design decisions. A benefit of working on mobile applications is that the development cycle tends to be relatively short, so it is likely that you will be able to revise an application's design when new technology emerges. However, whether it is the promise of more bandwidth or better devices, we never really know when the technology or device companies are going to deliver.

Long-term trends to look for in mobile technology are those that may transform the nature of mobile computing, like digital networks. Two technologies that have long been talked about are likely to impact mobile application development and subsequent user interface design quite substantially. The first is the long awaited 3G mobile network. The 3G network has undergone several evolutionary cycles even before it was launched. In essence, to the user the 3G network will mean three things: 1) an always-on connection; meaning the user will no longer have to log on to access the mobile network (akin to DSL or T1 Internet connectivity compared to modem dial-in); 2) faster transfer of information with data rates from 128–384 kbits, depending on how stationary a user is (current 2G digital networks are 9.6–14.4 kbps); and 3) the new rich complex applications the previous two listed technological innovations enable (e.g., multimedia, voice interactive, transactional, and other applications).

The second mobile technology that may greatly impact the way mobile devices interact in our lives are spontaneous local area wireless networks. Spontaneous local area wireless networks (e.g., Bluetooth and WiFi) allow enabled disparate devices to spontaneously form a wireless network when they come within close proximity to one another. For example, a user carrying a properly equipped PDA within range of a similarly equipped printer at a customer's office would be able to print documents directly from the PDA to that printer without any wired connection. Proponents of such networks claim that tiny computers will be ubiquitous in our society (offices, homes, and public areas), where spontaneous local area wireless networks will be forming and unforming constantly all over the world. The actualization of this vision could dramatically change the opportunities for mobile computing and would undoubtedly touch the user interface as well.

Another facet of fighting the hype is limiting the publicity, either internal or external to a company, that mobile applications will solve all ills. That is not the case. Mobile is another information channel for limited use cases. It is not a transforming information channel like the Web. We are highly unlikely to all leave our desks and wander aimlessly amid nature, city streets, or our homes working on mobile devices purely because we can. The mobile context is a medium to do certain types of actions in certain types of environments. Constraining your product design to these specific actions and environments will be key to actual and perceived success. Explaining these realities to upper management, customers, investors, and other principal stakeholders is critical in guiding mobile development objectives.

5.3.10   Heuristic 10: Basic UI Principles Still Apply

As the other heuristics imply, mobile devices are not reincarnations of the PC. Therefore, UI lessons learned for the PC need to be *adapted* for the mobile form factor, not applied verbatim. The other heuristics discuss the adaptations needed; however, successful mobile UI design must adhere to the universal UI principles that still apply. Some of these principles are: 1) consistency; 2) simplicity and efficiency; 3) learnability and discoverability; 4) robustness and reliability; 5) context awareness; 6) appropriate usage metaphors; 7) other basic visual design concepts (logical grouping, spacing, and so on); and 8) usability testing. What needs to be considered is how basic UI principles are applied to the mobile domain. Designers need to determine which principles increase in importance in mobile situations, and which principles need to be modified for mobile applications.

Consistency could be considered the gold standard of UI heuristics. However, the rapid pace of mobile development compared to traditional projects leads to significant challenges in maintaining interface consistency. Layout and design, terminology and navigation, and the overarching interaction metaphor used all need to remain consistent, both within applications and between applications of a common family.

Interface design standards can provide comprehensive guides for consistency in large development scenarios. It is very difficult even with a few developers to maintain consistency without some standardization. As teams and projects get larger, standards for component interface elements become a necessity rather than a designer luxury. These standards serve as the baseline from which creativity can start, rather than forcing each developer to reinvent the wheel. There is no greater threat to perceived usability than obvious inconsistency in application look and feel.

Simplicity and efficiency is a UI principle not likely to be ignored by mobile designers; however, it is a common first reaction of development to try to implement entire large complex applications into mobile devices instead of shedding features. Some lessons have been learned by teams moving from desktop to Web; however, the transition to mobile is a much longer journey. Many of the heuristics presented here are related to the limitations in mobile design space that require simplicity and efficiency (e.g., minimize data entry, every pixel counts). The mobile application designer's job is not just creating simple and efficient designs, but also to communicate this necessity to the developers (also see "Heuristic 9: Fight the Hype").

Learnability and discoverability take on greater importance in the mobile context, given limited exposure, use cases, and small interfaces. Therefore, anticipating users' needs is a more important challenge than in traditional large-display application design. Affordances for discovering features need to be more creative. And help information needs to be less cumbersome than in traditional environments. Every page should give the user some "instant gratification" in information or functionality that outweighs the cost of the download time.

The *robustness and reliability* of mobile applications is perhaps the most critical characteristic. Mobile users are likely to have short attention spans given the mobile context. Anything less than a very reliable and robust application is likely to lead the mobile user to a different path. Design does not directly impact reliability of applications; however, requirements from design could indirectly impact the complexity of the technology and ultimately, the performance of the application. Anything design can do to aid robustness and reliability should be considered.

Context awareness also assumes greater importance in mobile applications. Like other UI principles, this issue is exacerbated by the limited screen real estate of a mobile device. However, it may be of greater importance given the mobile contexts. An on-the-go user can easily be interrupted or otherwise purposely pause interaction with an application. Returning attention to the application either requires memory of context, or some easily visible or retrievable context information.

The *usage metaphor* of the desktop concepts dominates the computer world. Mobile application development needs to consider if the desktop metaphor is the appropriate carryover for their scenarios. Thus far, it appears that the desktop continues its sway over mobile applications. At least this is true from an enterprise perspective, where most mobile applications are related to an existing desktop or Web application. The transfer of knowledge from one platform to the next is the most important factor for metaphor consideration in this environment. However, applications developed specifically for mobile devices and without a link to a desktop application may want to consider a different metaphor. This exploration of a new mobile UI metaphor is only recently possible. Early mobile technology (e.g., WAP) allowed only a "list" metaphor (if that can even be considered a metaphor).

Other *basic visual design concepts* such as logical grouping by importance and frequency and including sufficient spacing need to be followed. Mobile design does not relax the need to follow these basic principles of visual design. As discussed in these heuristics, many of the issues gain in importance. Despite the change in the design medium, the challenge is still information design as much as it is interaction design. The flow of one "page" to the next and maintaining the user's understanding and attention are old standbys of visual design. Despite smaller spaces, narrower bandwidth, and new and different interaction mechanisms, basic visual principles in information design will still form the baseline of all your mobile designs as well.

Usability testing is the penultimate task in interface design. It is impossible to validate designs without users. No effort to avoid testing with users has yet been successful. Either the market will dictate your success or failure with users implicitly, or formalized usability testing can do so explicitly. Choosing to perform usability testing within your own confines can greatly improve your product's consistency, learnability, discoverability, and many of the heuristics discussed here and elsewhere. It is an essential component to successful product development projects. Just because mobile applications are small and lightweight (if you have done your job right) does not mean that the same level of validation via usability testing is not necessary. To the contrary, evaluation is just as critical because the cost of a user error or an inefficient navigation flow is so high due to long download times.

Usability testing mobile applications with emulators has its pros and cons. Emulators run on a desktop, and provide the user with a high-fidelity simulation of the application. Testing can be run in a traditional usability lab, and screen capturing devices can be used to record the users' interactions. Testing with emulators allows for capturing data on the users' performance and understanding of the application's navigation structures, clarity, and efficiency. Subjective data can also be informative on the utility of the features and perceived usefulness of the application.

One should be cautious, however, in basing all usability assessments on emulator testing. Since the emulators run on a desktop and either access local files or utilize high speed Internet connections, one cannot capture the effects of the slow download time on users' performance and subjective ratings. For example, longer download time may adversely affect performance because the users may get distracted within their mobile contextual environment, or may simply forget information that was stored in their short term memory. Also, the environment may hinder performance. Low lighting conditions, noisy distractions, traffic, or whatever else the users may be faced with can all have effects on how well the user can interact with the mobile application. Subjective ratings can also be influenced by slow download time. Applications that are feature rich and aesthetically enhanced with graphics may test well on a fast emulator, but may annoy users in real-time environments when users are in a hurry to get the information they need or to perform some task. Subjective ratings can also be influenced by the hardware itself. The combination of text input, viewing the small displays, and software operation can reduce the users' overall satisfaction with the application.

Testing on live applications with the actual devices can provide performance, subjective, and very realistic anecdotal information. These tests can be effective to see if users can find, recite, or recall information while using a mobile application. One can also obtain subjective ratings, such as user satisfaction and perceptions of the utility of the application. These subjective ratings are actually more realistic than those captured via emulator testing, because any effects that a slow download time and hardware human factors have on these ratings would be captured. There is also the possibility to capture anecdotal information that may be caused by some environmental factors. This type of information can be difficult to anticipate from testing inside a usability lab. An additional benefit is that mobile applications are relatively easier to develop, compared to a traditional desktop application developed in, for example, C++. Therefore, testing live code does not necessarily imply that you are testing a product late in the development cycle.

Testing on live applications also has its difficulties. Without the aid of a screen capturing system, observation of user interaction is problematic. Having the users stand or sit still and pointing a video camera at the device can provide some degree of viewing, but the video quality is poor, and can be obscured if the user moves or shakes. Anchoring the device in a cradle can help, but this reduces the fidelity of the environment. It is possible to develop server-side tools to record user navigation and even errors, but this is costly, as development resources are needed.

One drawback, whether testing live applications or via an emulator, is that you are confined by the existing technology stack. For example, for phones, you are restricted to today's WML, HDML, or cHTML. For PDAs, you are restricted to HTML 3.2 or the subset used in Palm™ "Web clipping" applications. These restrictions prevent prototyping conceptual, "blue sky" designs. For future oriented designs, you will be better off using some other prototyping tool.

5.4 Conclusions

Mobile applications seem to be the next evolutionary step in consumer and enterprise software. While designing these applications has its challenges, traditional usability and UI design methodologies are still applicable. The design heuristics provided in this chapter should transcend continually changing mobile technologies and hardware. The future will no doubt bring new challenges, and much more research will be needed. With new technology comes the chance for design innovation, and ultimately the ability to provide users with what they want and need.

Chapter 6

A Development Process for Advanced User Interfaces of Wireless Mobile Devices

Aaron Marcus

6.1 Intoduction

This chapter describes a process for developing user interfaces for advanced mobile wireless devices, based on research, contextual analysis, and prototyping. The process is based on research conducted by Aaron Marcus and Associates, Inc. (AM+A). AM+A designed future wireless mobile device user interface concepts for Samsung Electronics (Korea) that combined the functions of mobile telephones and personal digital assistants (PDAs). AM+A first researched emerging technology, social/cultural/business concepts, and advanced user-interface design. Then, AM+A provided to Samsung a suite of ideas for usable, useful wireless mobile devices to incorporate into future products.

Developing user interfaces for advanced wireless, mobile devices, is a challenging process. The development process, as described in Marcus [Marcus, 2002], includes the following steps, some of which are parallel, many of which are iterative:

- Planning
- Research
- Analysis
- Design
- Implementation
- Evaluation
- Documentation
- Training

The challenge is to design the appropriate user-interface components for such devices. These components, as described in Marcus [Marcus, 2002], are the following:

- Metaphors
- Mental models
- Navigation

- Interaction
- Appearance

This chapter describes the process that Aaron Marcus and Associates, Inc., (AM+A) went through in developing advanced conceptual prototypes of advanced wireless mobile devices for Samsung Corporation (Korea). AM+A considers the process to have been a fairly complete and appropriate one. Fortunately, Samsung has permitted AM+A to share some of its experiences, for which the authors are grateful.

Samsung's corporate user interface (UI) design team sought to obtain from AM+A information about desirable product concepts for the US market in the form of research reports and partial product prototypes, as opposed to a specific finished product design. Samsung staff also wanted to understand better AM+A's user interface development process.

In late 2000, the User Interface Research and Development Department of Samsung Electronics Corporation asked AM+A to research market, technology, and UI techniques, and then to develop a catalogue of conceptual user interface designs for future wireless information devices (WIDs) in 2002 and 2003 that would emerge from mobile phones, but also incorporate other functions. These concepts would be used as a reference by the Samsung UI team and engineers as a basis for specific product implementation based on manufacturing and marketing requirements. This project involved research, user observation, brainstorming, scenario development, and prototyping. The entire user experience was to be considered, from performance to pleasure, and the entire US mobile market was AM+A's user base to study.

The results from this project were three 40- to 60-page research reports, a catalogue of nearly 100 product concepts, and an integrated interactive demo of selected concepts incorporated into a conceptual design for a WID that AM+A named "Mob-i." The "i" stands for both "information" and "identity." All of the designs shown are owned by Samsung, some with patents pending.

6.2 Project Details

6.2.1 Project Participants

Project participants included the authors and other staff members of AM+A. In addition, Samsung participants included Ms. SunWha (Amy) Chung, Manager, User Interface Team; Ms. Yoojin Hong, Designer; and Jennifer Kim, Designer, Software Laboratory, Corporate R+D Center, Samsung Electronics, Co., Ltd, Korea. AM+A also involved approximately a half dozen anonymous users.

6.2.2 Project Dates

This project began in early August 2000 and concluded in late December 2000. The project required approximately 30 hours per week of effort for Ball and Lee, and approximately ten hours per week of effort for Chen during that time, in addition to contributions from Marcus and other staff members of about fours total per week.

6.2.3 Design and Development Process

Researching the Wireless Future

As difficult as it is to make small "baby-face" (small display) devices usable, there is also the fundamental challenge of making them *useful*. To achieve both goals, we followed a user-centered design process that emphasized significant research, including studying potential users and including them in initial concept design activities.

During the first research phase, we analyzed three dimensions: cultural and market trends (particularly to learn from advanced product developments in Europe and Asia), emerging mobile technologies, and advanced user interface techniques. We obtained information primarily from Web sites, books, magazines, and conference proceedings. These resources informed us of consumer desires, technical feasibility, and usability. Our three 40- to 60-page analysis reports to Samsung identified markets and social settings, described most newly emerging technologies (including a glossary of terms), and discussed tradeoffs among strengths and weaknesses of specific technologies. Of note, we identified the desirability of a mix of mobile phone and PDA functions, mixed voice and graphical modes, and context-aware functions.

Observing Users To Discover Their Needs

A fourth dimension of research was direct observation of users, which gave us insight into how these functions and features might best be combined. To develop innovative products, you need to identify unmet needs and desires of users. Focus groups seemed unreliable, because users find it difficult to envision products they haven't encountered yet. Observation in the field would be necessary in order to fully understand users' mobile experiences. AM+A targeted a wide variety, but limited number, of users for contextual observation. During our research, we developed a matrix of likely markets and social settings that matched characteristics of our users to optimize our selections. Our eventual user set was limited by budget 1to approximately a half dozen individuals near our California location. We tried to maximize diversity of characteristics with a minimal set of users. Participants included a priest who used many high-tech gadgets, a male college student, a female high school student, a male professional commuter, and a female, single-parent entrepreneur.

We followed each user for one day of routine activities, especially "information use." We watched how the subjects not only used electronic sources like mobile phones and personal digital assistants, but also traditional resources like newspapers and sticky notes. We kept a running log in text and images and recorded unmet needs, inefficiencies, and information artifacts. Each user continued a similar observation, recording activities in a self-log on paper or via tape recorders that we provided each participant. We brought back all users for a group interpretation session.

Brainstorming and Prototyping

Following the research and strategy phase, we ran a series of structured brainstorming workshops. The user-observation activities inspired these workshops,

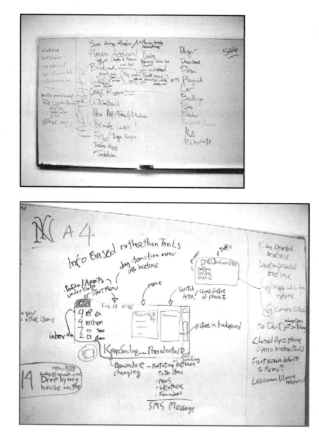

Figure 6.1   Concept-creation whiteboards

which we held with both the users and the client. Some user context examples are described later, in "Design Concepts Based on User Observation".

For each session, we listed and prioritized items, collected ideas on large stick-on notes, paper notes, electronic notes, and whiteboards. We organized all of them into folders organized by key ideas, and each folder had an "owner" who collected further contributions. Our whiteboards held the scope of problems to be solved, issues, half-formed ideas, and solutions (Figure 6.1). From these sessions, we were able to determine a product landscape that met the needs of the users we interviewed (Figure 6.2). The axes varied from simple to complex, from productivity to pleasure. The weighting of users seemed to confirm our de-emphasis on entertainment and pleasure solutions for the present time.

Analytical Framework

The next task was to develop a system of solutions based on insights from research. We created an analytical framework to help organize the complexity of users'

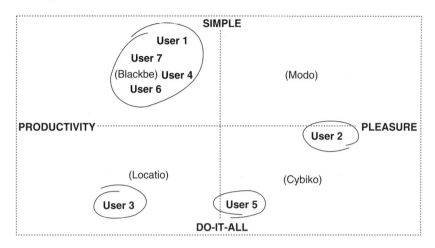

Figure 6.2   Product landscape with user-participant locations

behavior identified from merging those activities described in the literature. This framework is discussed later, in "Wireless Device Usage Space: an Analytical Framework."

Interactive Prototyping

Finally, we created an interactive prototype in Macromedia Flash to demonstrate the scenarios selected by Samsung. This prototype focused on concepts that involved more complex interaction or animation. All of these concepts were considered by AM+A and Samsung to fall in the targeted areas of medium complexity, productivity orientation, and usage areas identified earlier.

Concluding Steps

AM+A conducted design research, product strategy, and user observation to develop concept designs, which were varied, realistic, compelling, and detailed. As planned, Samsung would later determine which concepts to incorporate into specific manufactured products based on their assessment of engineering, manufacturing, and marketing requirements. Because we communicated extensively to Samsung staff through interim and final reports, meetings, and e-mail messages, Samsung's user interface design group also was able to observe and monitor continuously AM+A's process and progress. Through this frequent and detailed communication, especially via e-mail, Samsung could manage AM+A's efforts closely and learn details about AM+A's user-centered design process, thereby achieving Samsung's short-term and long-term goals.

6.3 Solution Details

6.3.1 Design Concepts Based on User Observation

Because of their small number (which fostered a "special group" bonding), and their location of our office nearby (which made it easier for users to participate in repeat interactions), the users were willing, enthusiastic, and helpful. As noted above, the user-observation activities inspired our brainstorming workshops, especially because users could contribute. Several of our design concepts were direct results of behavior that we observed. Two such examples are the following:

Figure 6.3 shows the personal organizer of a teenage girl, which shows extensive personalization and ornamentation. Intimate photos and memories, in addition to raw information, provide warmth as well as functionality. Based on these observations, we developed concepts for an effective user interface that would make Mob-i seem more personal.

Figure 6.4 provides evidence of a common problem. The user is receiving information by phone, which he is manually transferring to a paper appointment book. This kind of use is very difficult on phone–PDA combinations, for which the device must be moved away from the ear for hand-and-eye activity.

6.3.2 Wireless Device Usage Space: An Analytical Framework

The usage space that served as our analytical framework is shown in Figure 6.5. The framework structures many possible uses of wireless devices and proved helpful in planning the product concepts by enabling us to organize which uses to emphasize in our study.

Figure 6.3 Ornamented, personalized organizer of a teenage girl

Figure 6.4 Observation subject using phone and appointment book simultaneously

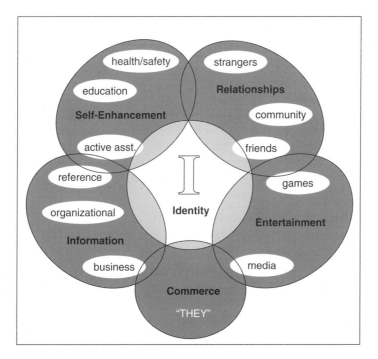

Figure 6.5   Usage spaces of wireless devices

Each of the framework's components is described below.

Information includes static *reference* information, such as weather reports, dictionaries, and entertainment listings. *Organizational* information includes all personal information management (PIM) functions. *Business* information supports specific professionals, such as a drug-interaction reference for doctors.

Self-Enhancement describes ways in which the device extends a user's normal capabilities. For example, young people in Finland call cell phones "Kanny," which implies "extension of the hand [Holstein, 1999]." *Active Assistant* functions include extending a user's memory or reinforcing a user's intentions. For instance, "FriendMinder," a project from Stanford Persuasive Technology Lab, encourages regular contact with loved ones [Fogg, 2000].

Health and Safety describes the ability of mobile devices to enhance safety through contact with emergency response teams or family.

Relationships refer to the way phones connect users. Mobile devices will become especially successful where they extend existing social protocols. Products like Cybiko [Cybiko], which are aware of the presence of other Cybiko units, allow users to connect to temporary *communities* of other users. For instance, these kinds of products are capable of enhancing intimacy between two people who wish to be in more constant contact through "presence" (see Figure 6.8).

Entertainment includes enjoyment of portable *media* such as music, astrology readings, and jokes, and *games* involving multiple users and location-based elements. These contents become particularly desirable in captive situations or for short bursts of spontaneous stress relief.

M-commerce refers to a variety of uses, including electronic money and e-coupons. The popularity of mobile devices will, in part, be catalyzed by viable commercial services. "They" refers to services being provided from the business world to the individual.

We proposed to Samsung that we emphasize functions and features that would assist most of these usage spaces, but would focus on performance and productivity rather than those that might be more frequently used for purely entertainment purposes, because these techniques were more likely to dominate early usage patterns.

6.3.3   Wireless Devices: The First Truly "Personal" Computers

Identity. The five usage spaces are centered around the *Identity* of the user. Due to the "always-with-you, always-on" nature of handheld devices, these devices can become knowledgeable over time about their owners. The "I" in Figure 6.5 represents the device's use as the seat of memory of the user.

The wireless information device should act as "cookies" do for Web surfing, providing persistent data and personalization. However, the WID will be able to do so over a broader spectrum of the user's life, because it will accompany the user wherever he or she goes. Memory of basic user information and more complex behavior patterns allows the device to reduce the amount of input required.

For example, if the WID can be involved in the m-commerce transaction of renting a car, the rental process can be shortened using the user's vehicle preferences. Devices can ultimately implement "deep personalization" [Brand]. If the WID knows that you are scheduled to travel to Chicago next week, it can offer you the weather in Chicago, so that you do not have to browse for it (see Figure 6.9).

6.3.4 The Promise of Mobile Computing

Handheld computers are more popular in social settings due to their low cost and great durability. We concentrated our design on user-oriented tasks rather than data-oriented ones, like checking stocks or surfing the Web. We also tried to focus Mob-i's purpose through segmenting the ways that people use information:

- *Creation*: Using authoring tools, such as a spreadsheet tool.
- *Gathering*: Picture-taking, filming, recording audio, gathering sensor input, and filling-in input forms (such as express-mail shipping that pick-up agents use).
- *Processing*: Organizing, manipulating, and interpreting information through applications and file managers.
- *Retrieval*: Accessing information from the Web, or from personal storage.
- *Communication*: Transferring information either to or from the device.

Mobile devices should excel at *communication* tasks; only the destination needs to be specified. They also may be made to perform adequately at *retrieval* tasks, like e-mail reading and Web surfing, and at *gathering* tasks, such as digital picture-taking. For instance, we emphasized information-gathering features because they present fewer input and output demands.

6.3.5 Two Design Philosophies: Specialized Use vs. Does Everything

Two distinct product-design philosophies compete in the vision of future WIDs. The *information-appliance* philosophy stresses the value of specialized devices. The *Swiss Army knife* approach assumes a single device with many uses. Based on our research reports and discussions with the client, we believe a middle path is correct. WIDs will provide access to high-value information and enable mobility-based tasks.

The challenge will be to identify what is essential immediately versus what can wait until a user accesses a desktop computer. We addressed this issue by letting users prioritize features themselves, letting them list each desirable function on a card. Each user's cards were taped together to form a long chain, which enabled everyone to visualize that the more functionality a device takes on, the more complex it becomes. Another way that we thought about the value-cost ratio of functions was by taking an inventory of the current mobile belongings of each user. We photographed and discussed the contents of their pockets, wallets, backpacks, and briefcases. Users and our team recognized the need for multiple tools and multiple content because of the lack of suitably designed, integrated approaches to their needs.

6.3.6 The Design Concept Catalogue

We provided Samsung with an illustrated catalogue of approximately 100 product concepts, each with a descriptive scenario and illustrations. In the catalogue, we demonstrated solutions to challenging but important situations, like creating appointments, using voice commands, and taking notes during a phone call. Some of these concepts are illustrated in Figures 6.6 through 6.11.

The catalogue is organized into system elements and users, which include the following:

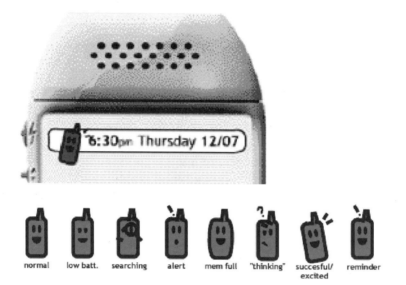

Figure 6.6 Affective personality. Mob-i has an engaging and expressive personality, which is shown through a status indicator in the title bar of every screen. The animated character shows signal strength, memory, battery life, reminders, etc. Mob-i's personality enables users to feel more attachment to their personal pocket assistants. Users can download new personalities, which load new images, phrases, and speech voices into the device

Figure 6.7 Detachable ear-piece. Mob-i's main body communicates to a wireless headphone-microphone via Bluetooth. This soft ear-bud, which pops out of the back of the device, can be worn comfortably in the ear like a hearing aid. The separate ear attachment allows the user to perform visual tasks without using a speaker phone or trailing wire. Wearing the ear-bud, users can be notified of calls and reminders privately and silently

Figure 6.8 Relationship room. Each person in the address book has an easy-to-enter relationship room, a one-to-one chat, scribble, and photo area. Users can exchange personal messages with this person in real-time, or leave them notes. These rooms eventually form a scrapbook of memories and/or a data/transaction archive

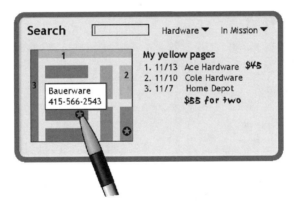

Figure 6.9 My yellow pages. Jack is getting repairs done by a carpenter. He will need to call back in a few days to see if the work is done and then will need to see the map again to remember how to get there. Mob-i maintains a history of regular businesses that he uses. He saves them to the "my yellow pages" list (e.g., the carpenter), separate from his personal address book

Figure   6.10   Location-based reminders.   Because   Mob-i   knows where Jack is, Mob-i can help him to remember to do something when he is at a good place to do it. Jack used to leave himself messages on his home answering   machine,   but   now   he leaves messages for himself on Mob-i and Mob-i reminds him

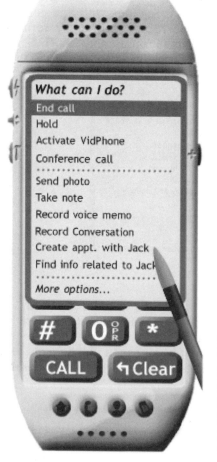

Figure 6.11 Activities during calls. The What-can-I-do? button allows the user to perform common tasks during a phone call. For instance, if the user is talking to Jack, the menu is adapted to include shortcuts for making an appointment with Jack and looking up Jack's address

- System
  - Metaphor
  - Front page
  - Tools and interruptibility
  - Information retrieval
  - Context awareness
  - Space saving
  - Multimodal interface
  - Personality

- Uses
  - Driving
  - Scanner
  - Note taking
  - Smart reminder
  - Visual voice messages
  - People visual phone
  - Telephone assistant
  - E-wallet
  - Smart yellow pages
  - Information gateway

Each of these topics appears with descriptions, brief scenarios, and visual sketches illustrating the ideas. Two examples of scenarios are the following:

Jill extensively uses Mob-i to jot down notes and reminders. She loves the fact that Mob-i helps her to store, remember, and organize these bits of information so that she no longer has to keep track of loose scraps of paper.

Busy Jack arrives home from work after stopping off to do some grocery shopping. He has a lot to take care of now that he's home: call his old friend; pay his bills and balance his checkbook; finish a few e-mails; take out the garbage; update his address book; and be reminded of things to bring from home the next morning. Previously, Jack left himself messages on his home answering machine, but now he leaves messages for himself on Mob-I, and Mob-i reminds him of them.

Because of the proprietary nature of the content, only a small reproduction of two pages may be shown (Figure 6.12). Samsung staff was able to review each concept, discuss them with us, and decide which should be carried further into a more finished concept. Although AM+A designed a physical form to embody the screen displays, most of the effort went into the screen displays (i.e., the metaphors, mental models, navigation, interaction, and appearance, including use of sound). The hard body of the device was assumed to house a camera as well as a removable wireless ear piece (with microphone) in the device's back, which the user could wear (see Figure 6.7).

6.3.7   Input and Output Limitations

Mobile devices with "baby-faces" have limited-size displays and tedious text input. These constraints forced us to consider alternative solutions, which included the following:

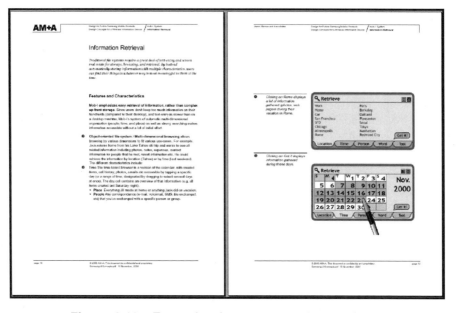

Figure 6.12   Example of concept catalogue pages

- *Contextual awareness.* Mobile devices can use techniques to contextualize the users input. By taking advantage of understanding the user's context, the device can automatically assist the user as much as possible, thereby saving time and the need for explicit input. For instance, the phone can automatically default to dialing a friend's work number during normal working hours in his/her own time zone. On evenings and weekends, the device can default to dialing a home number. If the device can go further and indicate the "presence" of the person to be called (e.g., available, in-a-meeting, driving), then possibly a call won't even be necessary (see Figure 6.11).
- *Location Awareness.* Location awareness is enabled by the use of GPS and Bluetooth technologies. User interface designers focusing on interaction soon will be able to utilize knowledge of a user's location as a way to aid usability. A helpful device can facilitate task completion by reminding a user, at the appropriate time and place, when he or she can do a certain task (see Figure 6.10).
- *Time-shifting.* Mob-i supports new modes of mobile work by providing a "start now, finish later" approach. For instance, users might simply mark each message as "Reply at Home," "Reply at Office," or "Print out at Office," etc. When they reach that location, they will be prompted to complete these partially finished tasks.

6.4 Post-Project Results

After the project was completed, AM+A representatives were able to present in person AM+A's findings, its development process, and its partial-product prototypes in the form of an interactive demo and PowerPoint lectures to Samsung's staff in Korea. The form of these presentations enabled Samsung staff to easily translate them into Korean and present them to engineering and marketing management. Samsung's user interface design manager and the project manager were satisfied with the results and felt that Samsung's development and technology transfer goals had been achieved.

One measure of the success of AM+A's participation was that Samsung felt comfortable enough to show AM+A's demo in Samsung's product exhibit booth at CHI 2001, which hundreds of user interface design professionals visited, including those of mobile device manufacturers. In addition, Samsung staff agreed to co-present a lecture about this project with AM+A at a special-interest group meeting at CHI-2001 attended by approximately 200 attendees. Finally, Samsung permitted AM+A to publish a featured cover story article about the project in the pages of ACM SIGCHI's *Interactions* magazine.

In retrospect, with more time on the project, AM+A would have explored more radical combinations of functions and other, more varied user scenarios, especially in the entertainment area. From AM+A's research, the teenage market seemed, to be a likely area for product innovation.

From Samsung's point of view, it would have been better to be able to station a Samsung staff member at AM+A's office in order to acquire a better understanding of AM+A's terminology, principles, and methods. Ricoh, in Tokyo, Japan, sponsored a similar kind of project with AM+A in past years. For that project, Ricoh sent one staff person to work in AM+A's offices for approximately three months while he worked on a joint project. That staff person was able to take back significant knowledge that was shared with Ricoh's user interface design staff. Such relationships help to augment technology transfer.

6.5 Acknowledgments

The authors wish to acknowledge the support and participation of Ms. SunWha (Amy) Chung, Manager, User Interface Team, and Ms. Yoojin Hong, Designer, Software Laboratory, Corporate R+D Center, Samsung Electronics, Co., Ltd, Korea. The authors wish also to acknowledge the staff of AM+A who contributed to the success of the project. This chapter is based significantly on [Marcus and Chen, 2000].

The author gratefully acknowledges the substantial contributions of the following to the work described in this chapter: Mr. Eugene Chen, Director of Design/Analysis; Mr. Luke Ball, Designer/Analyst; and Ms. Junghwa Lee, Designer/Analyst.

6.6 References

Brand, S. The Media Lab. MIT Press Cambridge.

Cybiko, Inc. http://www.cybiko.com. Reviews are at www.cybla.com.

Fogg, B.J., et al. (2000). http://hci.stanford.edu/captology. Stanford Persuasive Technology Lab.

Holstein, W.J. (13 December 1999). Moving beyond the PC. *U.S. News & World Report* 50.

Marcus, A. (Sep/Oct 2002). Dare We Define User-Interface Design? Fast Forward Column, *Interactions*. 31–36.

Marcus, A., and Chen, E. (Jan/Feb 2002). Design of Future Wireless Devices. *Interactions*. 34–45.

URLs (some with annotation)

Advanced Traveler Information Systems Committee.
    http://www.sae.org/technicalcommittees/atishome.htm

American National Standards Institute. http://www.ansi.org/

AnyWhereYouGo. News and discussion on both technological and business trends in the wireless industry. http://www.AnyWhereYouGo.com/.

AngelBeat. See Untethered: trends and definitions for wireless Web and mobile Internet by this solutions provider. http://www.angelbeat.com/

BlackBerry. http://www.blackberry.net/

Handspring: makers of Visor and Treo. http://www.handspring.com/

i-Appliance Association. http://www.i-appliance.org/

International Standards Organization homepage. http://www.iso.ch/

Kyocera Wireless Products. http://www.kyocera-wireless.com/

Motorola. http://www.motorola.com.

Nokia USA. http://www.nokia.com/main.html

OnHand Watch PC. World's smallest computer on the wrist, with interactive demo.

Palm plus peripherals. http://www.palm.com

Palm accessories. One of the best sites to support Palm users according to the New York Times, Feb. 1999. http://www.palmgear.com/

Samsung Electronics Products: mobile division.
    http://samsungelectronics.com/mobile_phone/mobile_phone_index.asp

The Standard's Wireless News. http://thestandard.com/wireless

Symbian. Worldwide wireless platform. http://www.symbian.com/

Unstrung. Industry-specific news and views. http://www.unstrung.com/

Voice: IBM Voice Systems. Info about voice and speech recognition.
    http://www-4.ibm.com/software/speech

Voice: Lernout and Haupsie. Info about voice and speech recognition.
    http://www.lhsl.com/

WAP Forum. Information on the wireless Web protocol.
    http://www.wapforum.org/

ZDNet: Handhelds Guide.
    http://www.zdnet.com/pcmag/filters/guide/0,10172,6001651,00.html

Index

abstract command, 63, 65
abstract command's priority, 66
abstract command's type, 65
accelerators, 17
alert types, 74
alerts, 73
application hierarchy, 125
application management, 75

Bluetooth, 112
Brew, 5, 8, 9, 13, 31
buttons, 64

canvases, 74
CDMA, 2, 8, 31, 59
choice groups, 70
cHTML, 6, 133
CLDC, 56
composite multimodal interaction, 87
configurations, 56
connectivity, 59
constraints, 73
consumer characteristics, 60
context awareness, 132
context-sensitive forms, 68
contextual information, 87
create a mock-up, 62
custom items, 72
customization, 110, 129

date-time field, 71
degrees of multimodality, 87
demographic segmentation, 4
derive application flow, 62
dialog, 33, 36, 38, 41–46, 49, 53, 81, 90–92, 94, 96, 101, 105
dialogue, 80, 81, 85
downloaded applications, 6, 11

emulators, 132

feature shedding, 110, 122
file formats, 12, 27
form items, 69
form layout, 68, 70
form pages, 117
forms, 68

3G, 130
game API, 58
game canvases, 74
gauges, 71
graphical user interface, 83
GSM, 2, 8, 30, 31, 59

help, 22, 30, 39, 40, 42, 43, 48, 50, 53, 66
high-level user interface components, 67
HTML, 6, 25, 80, 83, 87, 89, 90, 96, 101, 104, 106, 133

icons, 11, 17, 20, 75, 116
identifying the tasks, 61
input field, 2, 14, 16, 17, 19, 28, 96, 104, 105
input methods, 14, 17, 21, 28, 57, 110, 124
input modes, 15, 17, 21, 28, 80, 87, 91
interaction state, 94
intermittent interaction, 113
interoperability, 2, 93
item-specific abstract commands, 64

Java™ 2 Platform, Micro Edition (J2ME™), 55

key mapping, 12, 13

label-data display pages, 114
labels, 65
layout directives, 68

lists, 73
local area wireless networks, 130
localization, 17, 20, 28, 95
log in, 30, 35
login, 30
low-level user interface components, 74

map the tasks, 61
media formats, 7, 10, 27
MIDP application, 61
MIDP device requirements, 60
MIDP features, 57
mobile information device profile (MIDP), 9, 55–69, 72, 74–76
mobile media API, 59
modifiers, 73
multimodal interaction, 80
multimodal synchronization, 88
multitasking, 113

name of your application, 76
native applications, 7, 9, 13, 14, 28
navigation model, 124
network access, 6, 9, 22, 23
network connection, 20, 22, 24, 56
network resources, 6, 22

open mobile alliance (OMA), 5
optional packages, 57
over-the-air provisioning, 59

paired commands, 66
password, 30, 37, 47
predictable, 60
profiles, 56
progressive disclosure, 118

screen size, 11, 12, 20, 27, 110, 114, 124
screens, 58, 61
scrolling, 15–17, 20, 58, 65, 67, 72, 116–119

security, 59
sequential multimodal interaction, 87
series 60, 8
simultaneous multimodal interaction, 87
size issues, 76
SMS multimodality, 87
social interaction, 113
softkeys, 13–17
speech application language tags (SALT), 90
speech recognition, ix, 33–39, 44, 48, 49, 51, 79, 85, 90, 105
status indicators, 14, 17, 20
string and image items, 71

tabular display pages, 116
TDMA, 2
text boxes, 73
text fields, 70
text input, viii, 10, 13, 15, 17, 84, 85, 100, 133, 147

ubiquitous computing, 111
unimodal interaction, 87
usability testing, 132
using abstract commands, 63, 69

voice user interfaces, ix, 33, 37, 38, 51, 53, 85
VoiceXML, 85

WAP, 5, 10, 11, 25, 33, 84, 87, 132, 150
WiFi, 112
WML, 6, 10, 25, 84, 87, 91, 98, 106, 133

XHTML, 6, 10, 25, 83, 90, 91, 96, 100, 106
XHTML + VoiceXML, 91